Fall for CGP's Spelling practice this autumn!

Start Year 2 spelling with a bang with CGP's Daily Practice! We've rustled up a book that will ~~leaf~~ leave any spelling troubles far behind...

There's a page of brilliant spelling practice for every day of the autumn term, all expertly matched to the Year 2 curriculum.

With easy-to-follow examples and colourful illustrations, it's perfect for use at home or in class — but not advised for lighting bonfires!

What CGP is all about

Our sole aim here at CGP is to produce the highest quality books — carefully written, immaculately presented and dangerously close to being funny.

Then we work our socks off to get them out to you — at the cheapest possible prices.

Contents

☑ Use the tick boxes to help keep a record of which tests have been attempted.

Week 1
- ☑ Day 1 1
- ☑ Day 2 2
- ☑ Day 3 3
- ☑ Day 4 4
- ☑ Day 5 5

Week 2
- ☑ Day 1 6
- ☑ Day 2 7
- ☑ Day 3 8
- ☑ Day 4 9
- ☑ Day 5 10

Week 3
- ☑ Day 1 11
- ☑ Day 2 12
- ☑ Day 3 13
- ☑ Day 4 14
- ☑ Day 5 15

Week 4
- ☑ Day 1 16
- ☑ Day 2 17
- ☑ Day 3 18
- ☑ Day 4 19
- ☑ Day 5 20

Week 5
- ☑ Day 1 21
- ☑ Day 2 22
- ☑ Day 3 23
- ☑ Day 4 24
- ☑ Day 5 25

Week 6
- ☑ Day 1 26
- ☑ Day 2 27
- ☑ Day 3 28
- ☑ Day 4 29
- ☑ Day 5 30

Week 7
- ☑ Day 1 31
- ☑ Day 2 32
- ☑ Day 3 33
- ☑ Day 4 34
- ☑ Day 5 35

Week 8
- ☑ Day 1 36
- ☑ Day 2 37
- ☑ Day 3 38
- ☑ Day 4 39
- ☑ Day 5 40

Week 9

- ☑ Day 1 41
- ☑ Day 2 42
- ☑ Day 3 43
- ☑ Day 4 44
- ☑ Day 5 45

Week 10

- ☑ Day 1 46
- ☑ Day 2 47
- ☑ Day 3 48
- ☑ Day 4 49
- ☑ Day 5 50

Week 11

- ☑ Day 1 51
- ☑ Day 2 52
- ☑ Day 3 53
- ☑ Day 4 54
- ☑ Day 5 55

Week 12

- ☑ Day 1 56
- ☑ Day 2 57
- ☑ Day 3 58
- ☑ Day 4 59
- ☑ Day 5 60

Answers 61

Published by CGP

ISBN: 978 1 78908 830 4

Editors: Emma Clayton, Katherine Faudemer, Sarah Pattison, Claire Plowman, Joe Shaw

With thanks to Andy Cashmore and Juliette Green for the proofreading.

With thanks to Lottie Edwards for the copyright research.

Cover and Graphics used throughout the book © www.edu-clips.com

Printed by Elanders Ltd, Newcastle upon Tyne.
Based on the classic CGP style created by Richard Parsons.

Text, design, layout and original illustrations© Coordination Group Publications Ltd. (CGP) 2021
All rights reserved.

Photocopying this book is not permitted, even if you have a CLA licence.
Extra copies are available from CGP with next day delivery • 0800 1712 712 • www.cgpbooks.co.uk

How to Use this Book

- This book contains 60 pages of daily spelling practice.

- We've split them into 12 sections — that's roughly one for each week of the Year 2 Autumn term.

- Each week is made up of 5 pages, so there's one for every school day of the term (Monday – Friday).

- Each page should take about 10 minutes to complete.

- The words tested are suitable for the Year 2 English curriculum. New words and sounds are gradually introduced through the book.

- The pages increase in difficulty as you progress through the book.

- Answers can be found at the back of the book.

- Each page looks something like this:

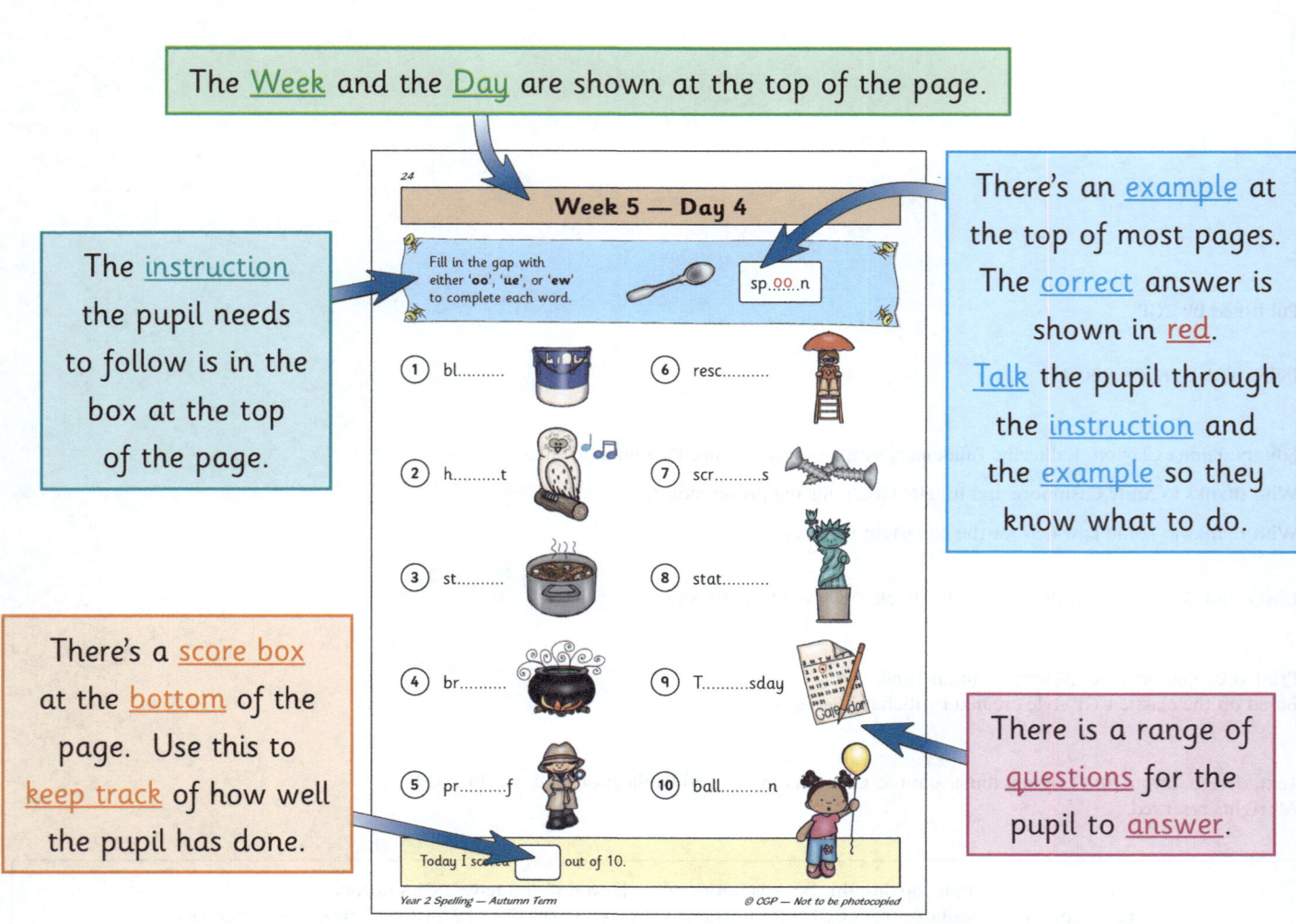

Week 1 — Day 1

Read each sentence. Circle the correct spelling of the word in bold.   Look at the **(dove)** / **duv**.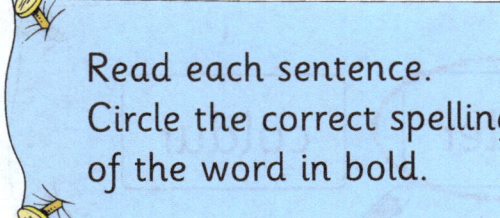

1) I **love** / **luv** going out.

2) **Giv** / **Give** me my bag.

3) We will be **above** / **abof** the clouds.

4) It's good to be **aktiv** / **active**.

5) We will walk for **twelf** / **twelve** miles.

6) Lots of animals **live** / **liv** on the mountain.

7) I **forgive** / **forgiff** you for splashing me.

Today I scored ☐ out of 7.

Week 1 — Day 2

Read each pair of words. Circle the word that is spelt correctly.

colder (circled) · coldur

1. softer · soffter

2. sikker · sicker

3. calmmer · calmer

4. sharper · sharpur

5. wildur · wilder

6. stronger · strongr

7. darkker · darker

8. quiker · quicker

Today I scored ▢ out of 8.

Week 1 — Day 3

Look at the pictures. Circle the correct letters to complete each word.

 m___n  (oo) / ue / ew

1  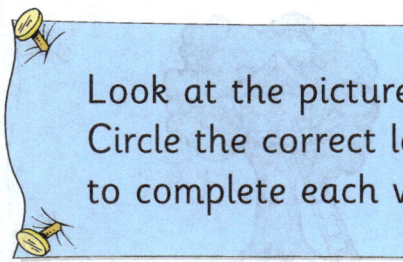 f___d   oo / ue / ew

2   fl___   oo / ue / ew

3   bl___   oo / ue / ew

4   gr___   oo / ue / ew

5  p___l   oo / ue / ew

6  r___t   oo / ue / ew

7  gl___   oo / ue / ew

Today I scored [ ] out of 7.

Week 1 — Day 4

Look at the pictures and read the sentences. Draw lines to match each sentence with the letters needed to complete the word in bold.

 Come to my **h___se**.

①  Bring some **t___s** with you.

②  **W___n** shall we play?

③  Will you **pu___** me on the swing?

④  He is **ca___ed** Kamal.

⑤  He is my **fr___nd**.

⑥  Let's have **so___** cake.

oy

me

ou

he

ie

sh

ll

Today I scored ☐ out of 6.

Week 1 — Day 5

Read each sentence. Write 'ir' or 'ur' to complete the words in bold.

We are all in a **wh.ir.l**.

1. A baby **g..........l** has been born.

2. We are going to **ch..........ch** on **Th..........sday**.

3. It will be my **f..........st** time.

4. Dad washes his **sh..........t** because it is **d..........ty**.

5. I wear my best **sk..........t** and **c..........l** my hair.

6. I do a **tw..........l**.

7. I watch the candle **b..........n**.

8. I'm so happy I could **b..........st**.

Today I scored ☐ out of 11.

Week 2 — Day 1

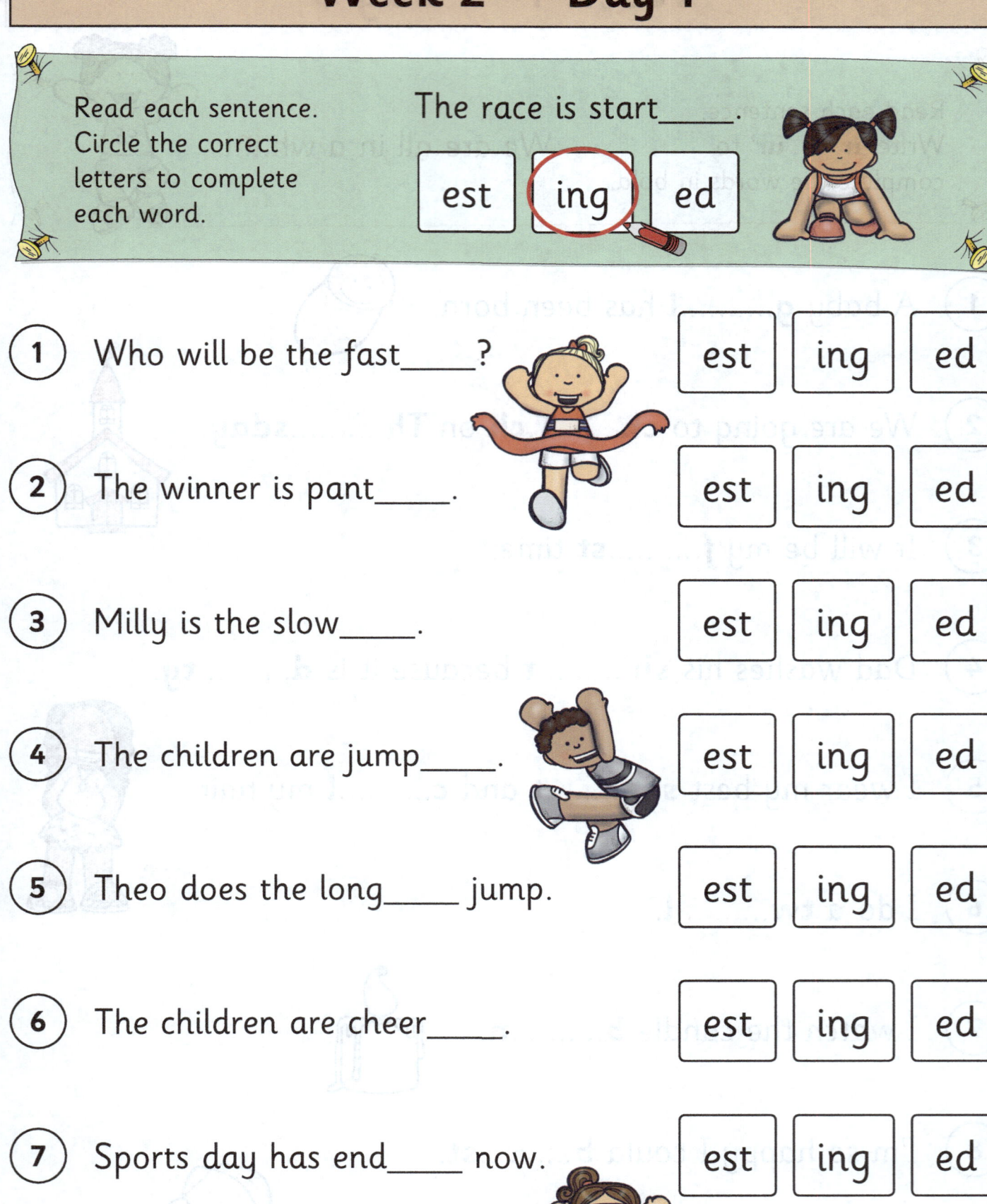

Read each sentence. Circle the correct letters to complete each word.

The race is start____.

est (ing) ed

1) Who will be the fast____?   est ing ed

2) The winner is pant____.   est ing ed

3) Milly is the slow____.   est ing ed

4) The children are jump____.   est ing ed

5) Theo does the long____ jump.   est ing ed

6) The children are cheer____.   est ing ed

7) Sports day has end____ now.   est ing ed

Today I scored ☐ out of 7.

Week 2 — Day 2

Read each pair of sentences. Tick the sentence where the word in bold is spelt correctly.

I am **five** years old. ✓
I am **fiev** years old. ☐

1. It is a sunny day in **June**. ☐
   It is a sunny day in **Joon**. ☐

2. The birds are singing a **toon**. ☐
   The birds are singing a **tune**. ☐

3. It's **time** to go. ☐
   It's **tyme** to go. ☐

4. We go up on the **dune**. ☐
   We go up on the **duen**. ☐

5. We are going to fly my **kyt**. ☐
   We are going to fly my **kite**. ☐

6. It will **ryse** up in the air. ☐
   It will **rise** up in the air. ☐

7. Then it will **diev** down again. ☐
   Then it will **dive** down again. ☐

Today I scored ☐ out of 7.

Week 2 — Day 3

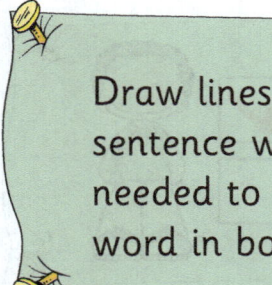

Draw lines to match each sentence with the letters needed to complete the word in bold.

What a j___! — aw

1. The **dinos___r** was hungry.

2. He found some **r___** meat.

ore

3. His **cl___s** were sharp.

4. He **t___** the meat.

or

5. He **cr___led** away.

aw

6. Then he **y___ned**.

7. I heard him **sn___**.

au

8. He slept until **m___ning**.

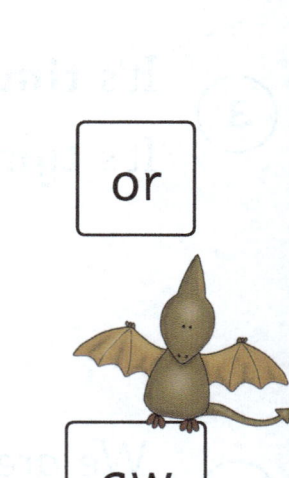

Today I scored [ ] out of 8.

Week 2 — Day 4

Read each sentence. Write the correct spelling of the word in bold.

This is my **stori**. ......story......

1. My **mummee** is the best. ....

2. I think she is **prety**. ....

3. She tells me **funnie** stories. ....

4. She mended my **teddie**. ....

5. She gave me a toy **poney**. ....

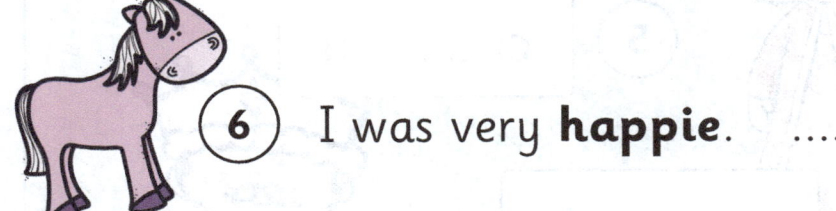

6. I was very **happie**. ....

7. After school, I **hurri** to see her. ....

8. She tucks me up in my **cosi** bed. ....

Today I scored ☐ out of 8.

Week 2 — Day 5

Look at the picture. Fill in the gaps in the words with '**ow**' or '**ou**'.

t..ow..n

1. fr.........n
2. l.........d
3. t.........er
4. cr.........ch
5. cr.........n
6. ....tside
7. ....ch
8. pr.........d

Today I scored [   ] out of 8.

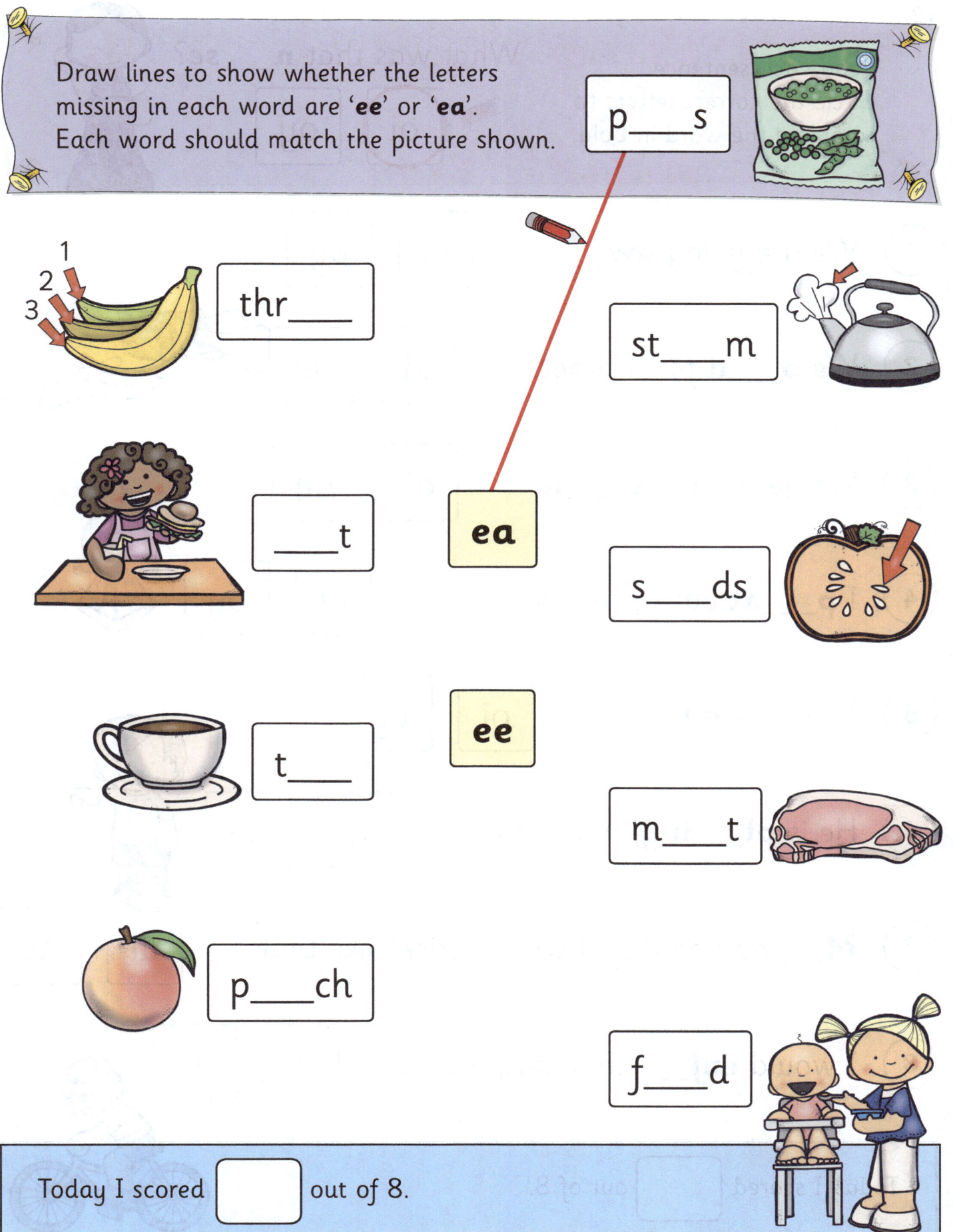

Week 3 — Day 2

Read each sentence. Circle the correct letters to complete the word in bold.

What was that **n___se?** (oi) oy

1. We are going **aw___**.   ai   ay
2. We **p___d** for a ticket.   ai   ay
3. We get on the **tr___n**.   ai   ay
4. I **p___nt** out of the window.   oi   oy
5. I can see a **b___**.   oi   oy
6. He is **pl___ing** on his bike.   ai   ay
7. **M___be** one day, I will do tricks like that.   ai   ay
8. I would **enj___** that very much.   oi   oy

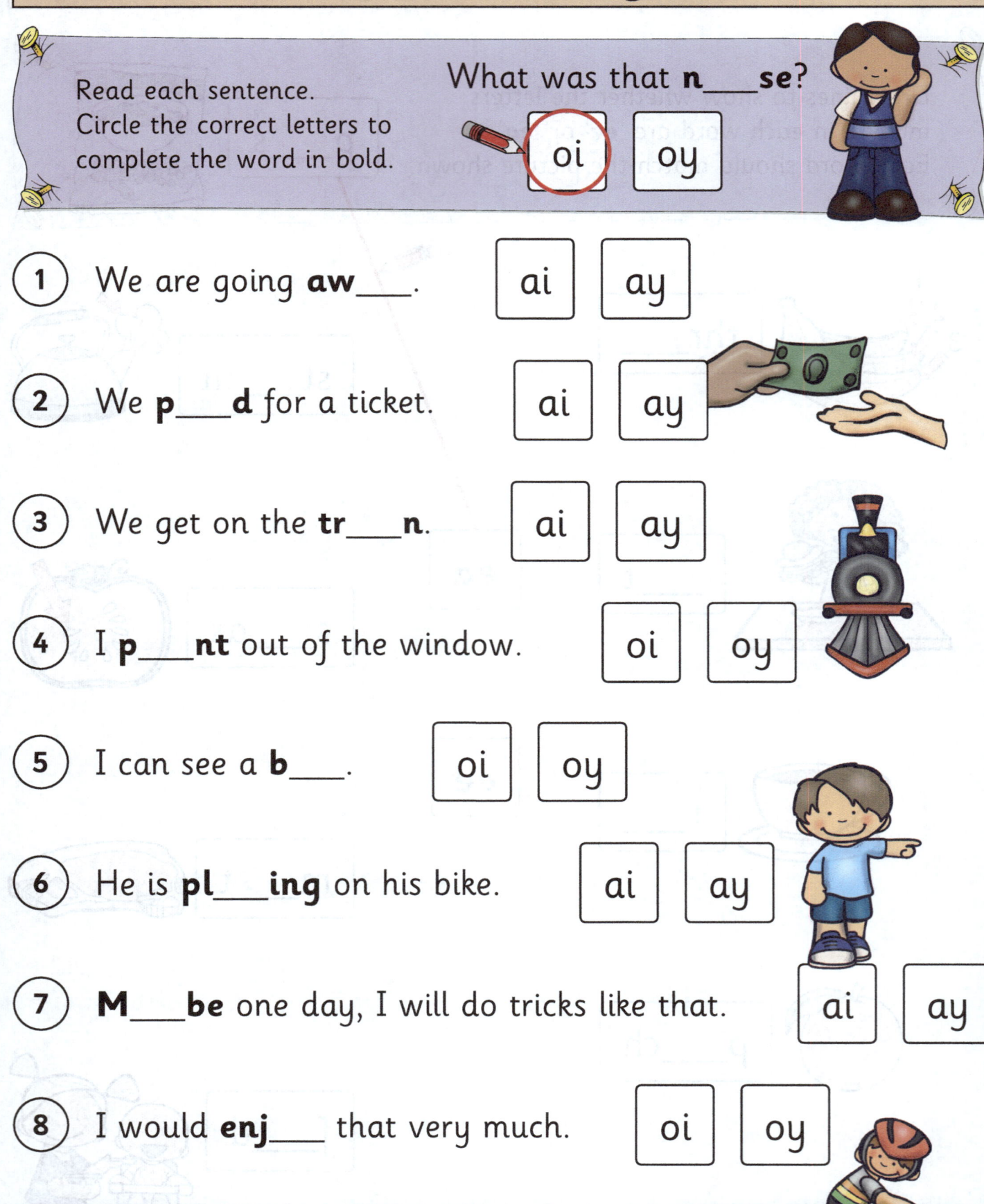

Today I scored [ ] out of 8.

Year 2 Spelling — Autumn Term

Week 3 — Day 3

Read each sentence. Underline any words in bold that are spelt correctly. Circle any words in bold that are **not** spelt correctly.

I <u>wish</u> I had my (**lunsh**).

1. We went on a **bowt**.

2. We could see lots of **fish**.

3. **Thenn** I saw a **shark**.

4. It was **sutch** a **shock**.

5. It **opened** its **mowth**.

6. It had **charp teeth**.

7. **There** was a **crashe**.

8. I **throo** it one of my **chips**.

9. It **arched** its back and swam off with a **splach**.

Today I scored ☐ out of 16.

Week 3 — Day 5

Look at the pictures. Each word has been spelt incorrectly. Write the correct spelling on the line next to it.

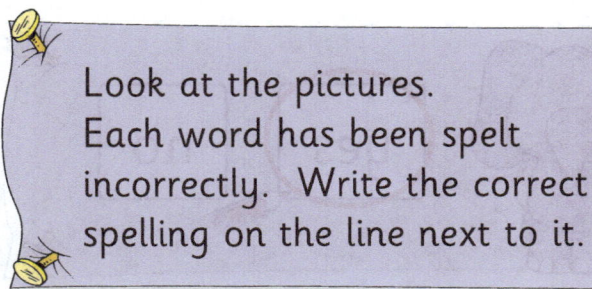

dride ..dried..

1. pigh ....

2. hyde ....

3. smiel ....

4. nite ....

5. shighn ....

6. hie ....

7. cryed ....

8. tite ....

Today I scored ☐ out of 8.

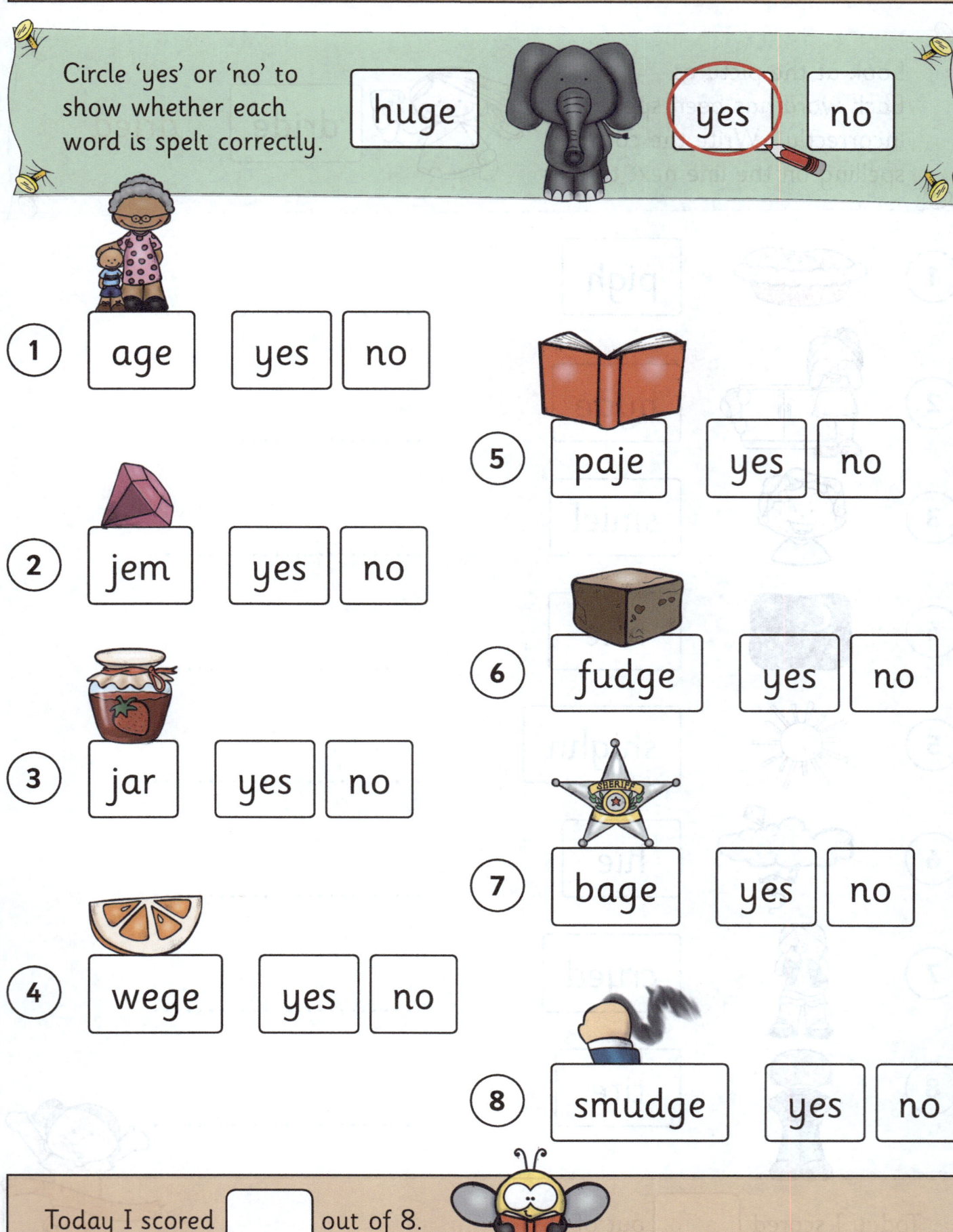

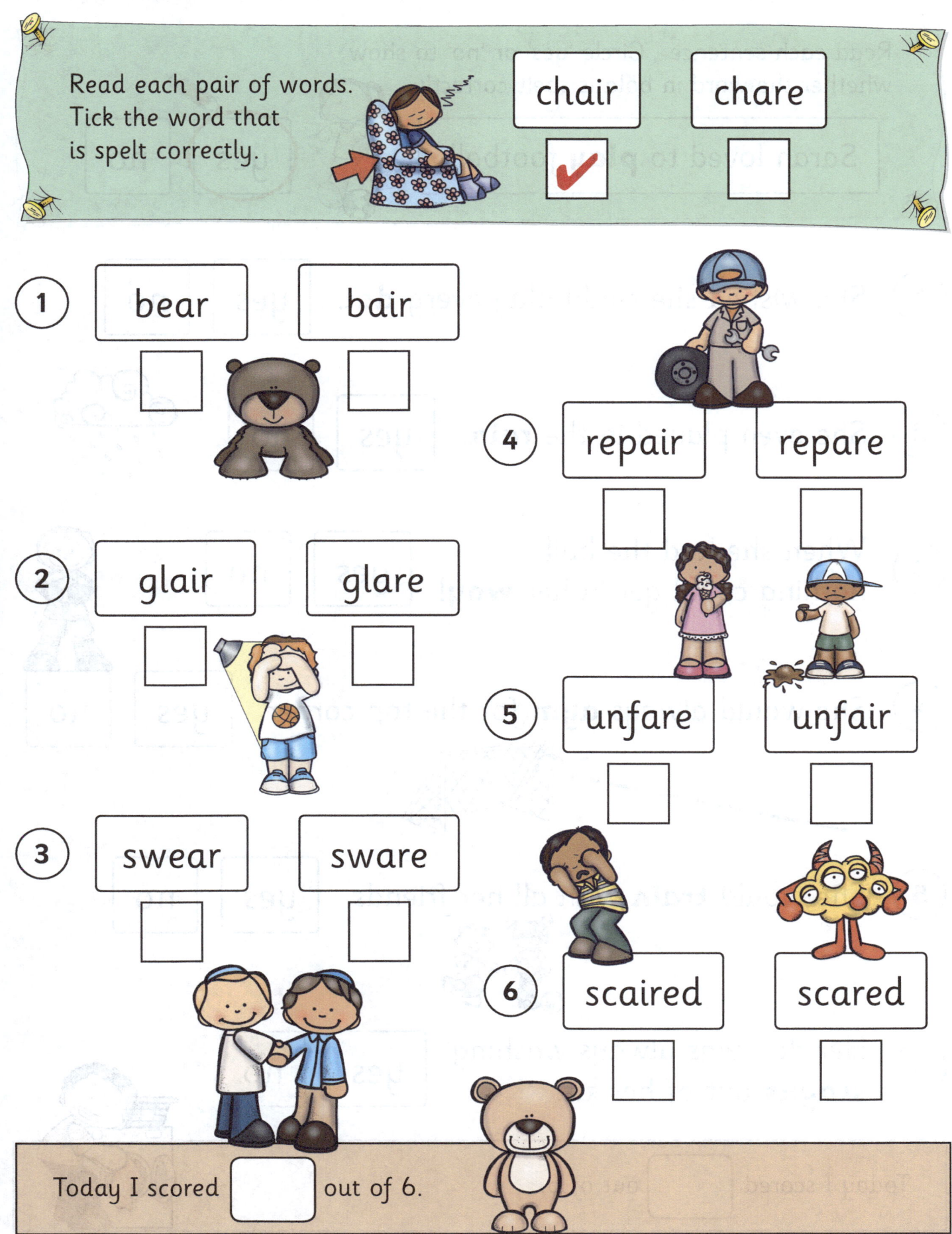

Week 4 — Day 3

Read each sentence. Circle 'yes' or 'no' to show whether the word in bold is spelt correctly.

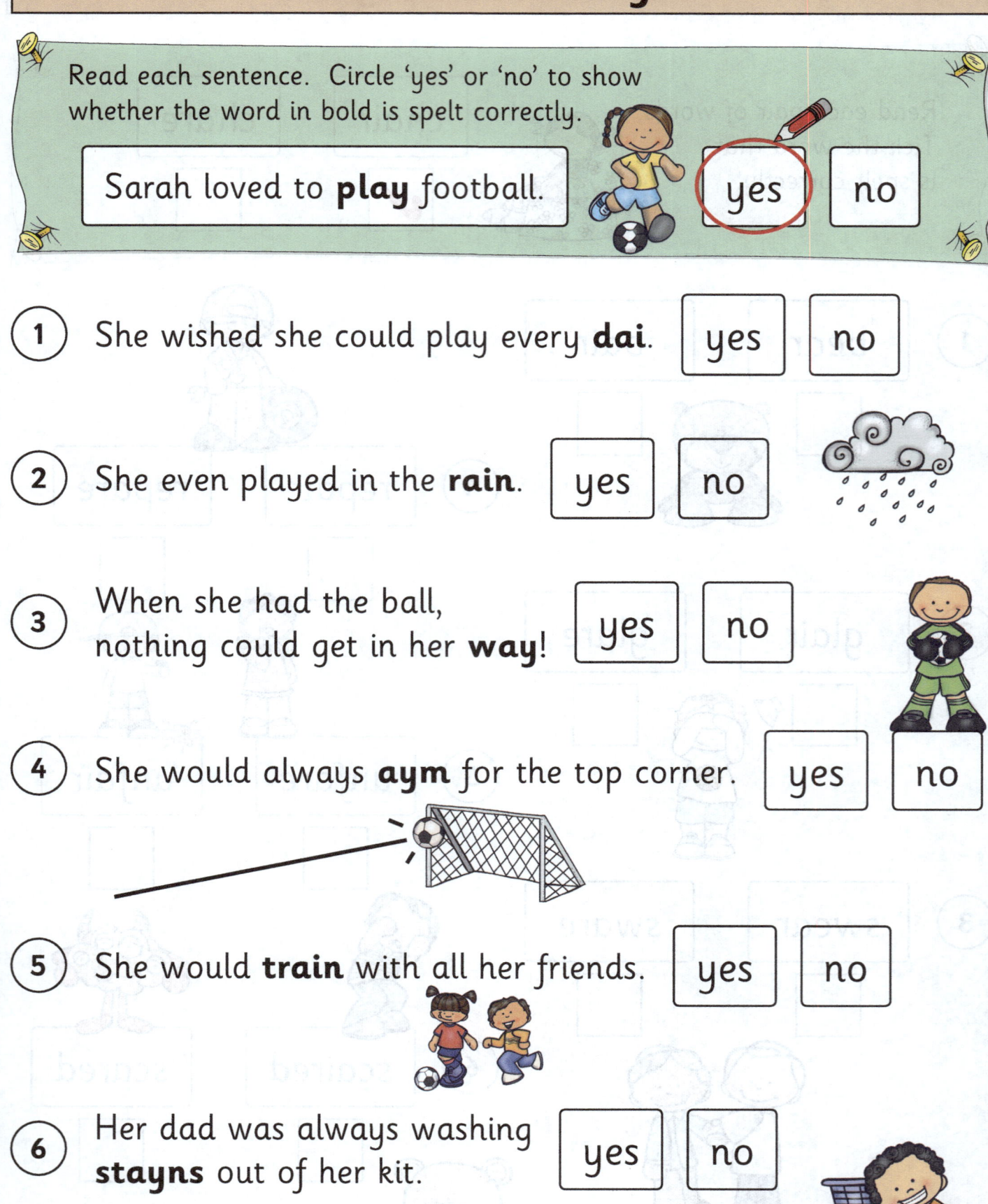

Sarah loved to **play** football. (yes) no

1) She wished she could play every **dai**. yes no

2) She even played in the **rain**. yes no

3) When she had the ball, nothing could get in her **way**! yes no

4) She would always **aym** for the top corner. yes no

5) She would **train** with all her friends. yes no

6) Her dad was always washing **stayns** out of her kit. yes no

Today I scored ☐ out of 6.

Year 2 Spelling — Autumn Term

Week 4 — Day 4

Week 4 — Day 5

Read each sentence. Circle the correct spelling of the missing word.

Isaac went for a _____.   (jog)   gog

1. Holly loved her new _____.   sledge   slege

2. The hose had a _____.   bulge   buldge

3. Liv was able to _____ the ball.   dodge   doge

4. The cat was _____.   ginger   jinger

5. I need to _____ my socks.   chandge   change

6. The food is in the _____.   frige   fridge

Today I scored ☐ out of 6.

Week 5 — Day 1

Colour the picture next to the word that is spelt correctly.

ice 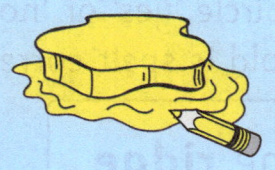   ise

1. rase    race

2. noice    noise

3. spise    spice

4. slice    slise

5. chanse 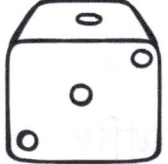   chance

6. cheese 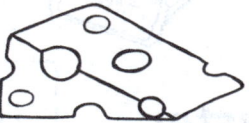   cheece

Today I scored ☐ out of 6.

Week 5 — Day 2

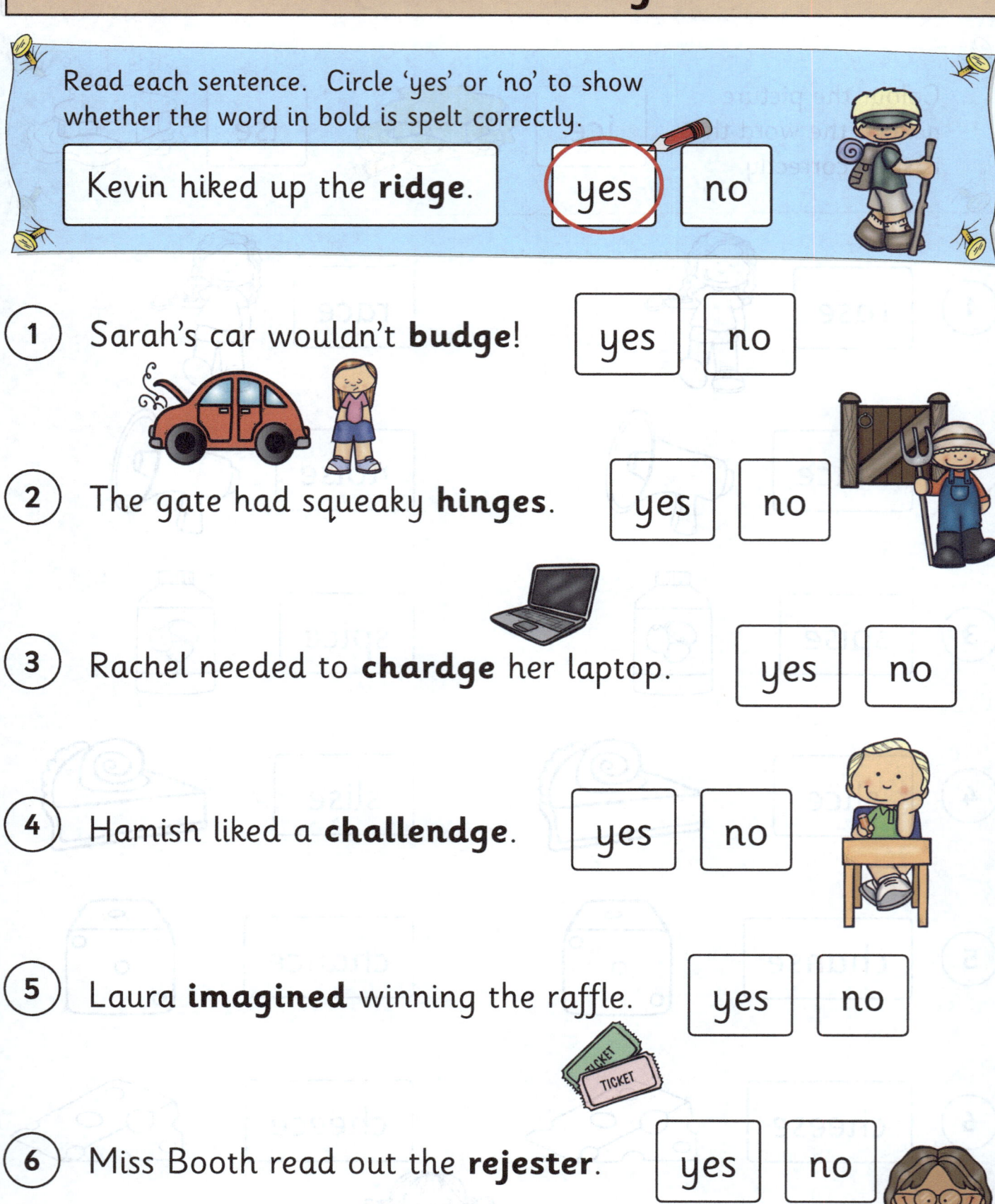

Read each sentence. Circle 'yes' or 'no' to show whether the word in bold is spelt correctly.

Kevin hiked up the **ridge**.   (yes)   no

1. Sarah's car wouldn't **budge**!   yes   no

2. The gate had squeaky **hinges**.   yes   no

3. Rachel needed to **chardge** her laptop.   yes   no

4. Hamish liked a **challendge**.   yes   no

5. Laura **imagined** winning the raffle.   yes   no

6. Miss Booth read out the **rejester**.   yes   no

Today I scored ☐ out of 6.

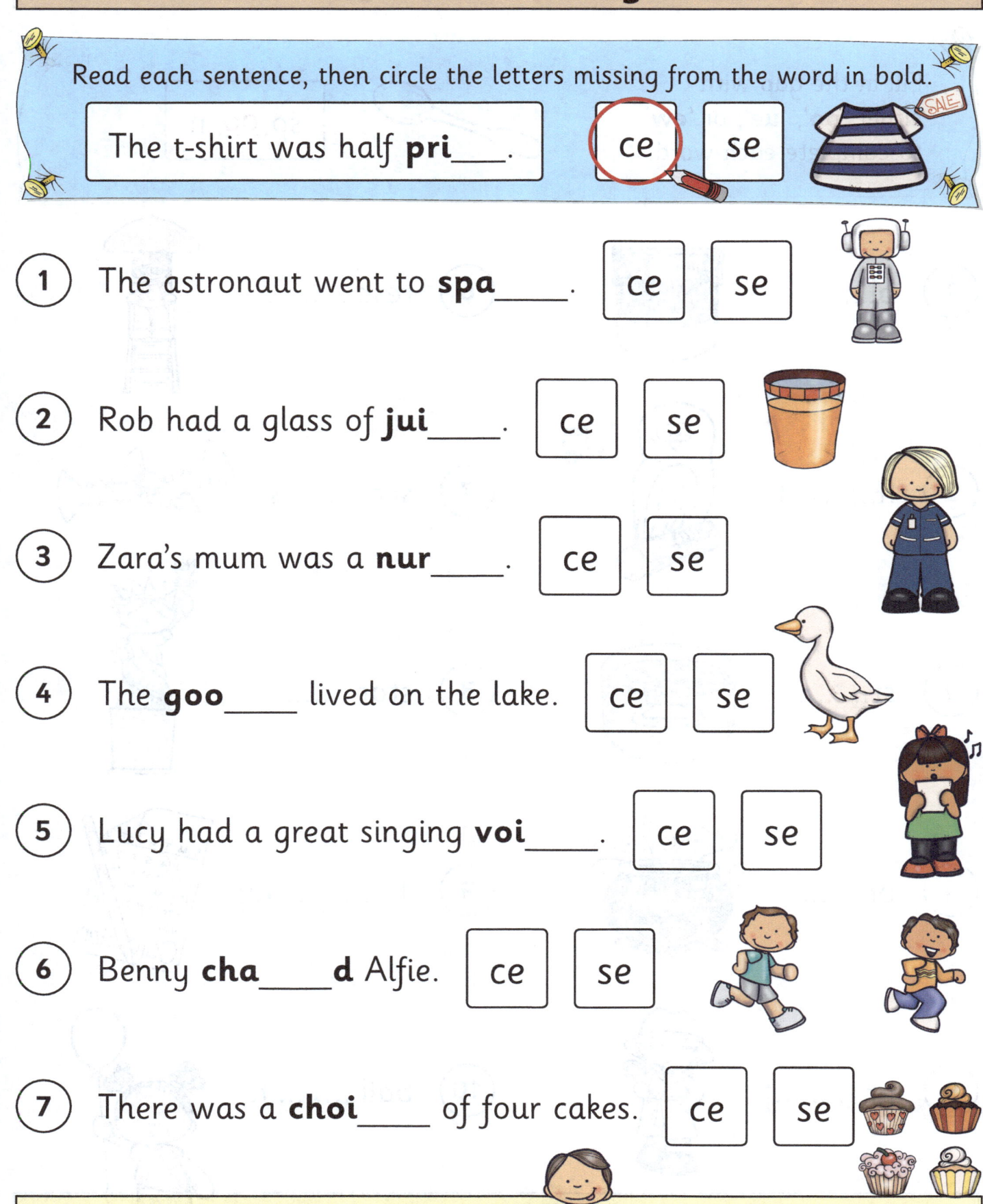

Week 5 — Day 4

Fill in the gap with either '**oo**', '**ue**', or '**ew**' to complete each word.

  sp..oo..n

1) bl..........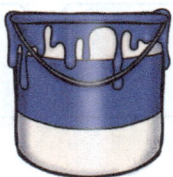

2) h..........t

3) st..........

4) br..........

5) pr..........f

6) resc..........

7) scr..........s

8) stat..........

9) T..........sday

10) ball..........n

Today I scored ☐ out of 10.

Week 5 — Day 5

Draw lines to match the words to the correct missing letters. Each word should match the picture shown.

bu___et — ck

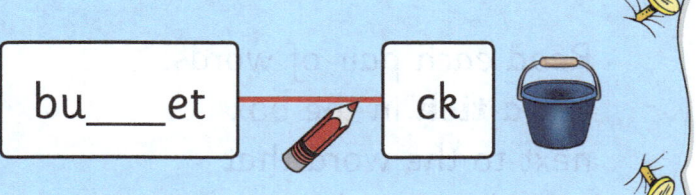

1 hoo___

2 blo___s

3 ___rutch

4 pa___ed

5 arcti___

6 chi___en

7 bar___ing

8 cho___olate

c

ck

k

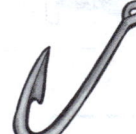

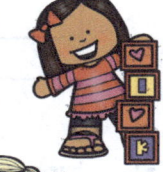

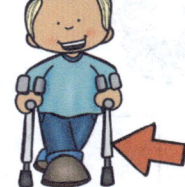

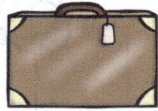

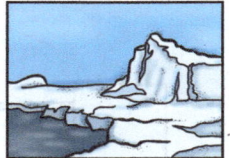

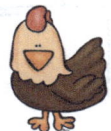

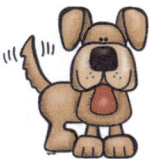

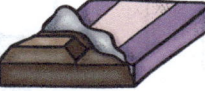

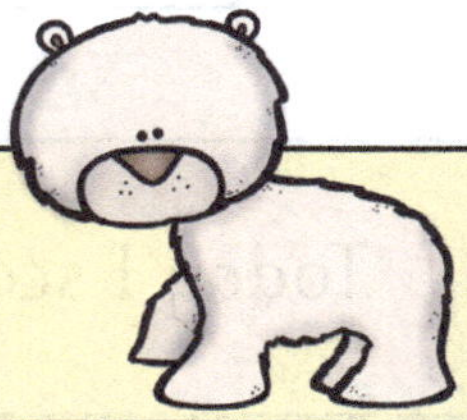

Today I scored [ ] out of 8.

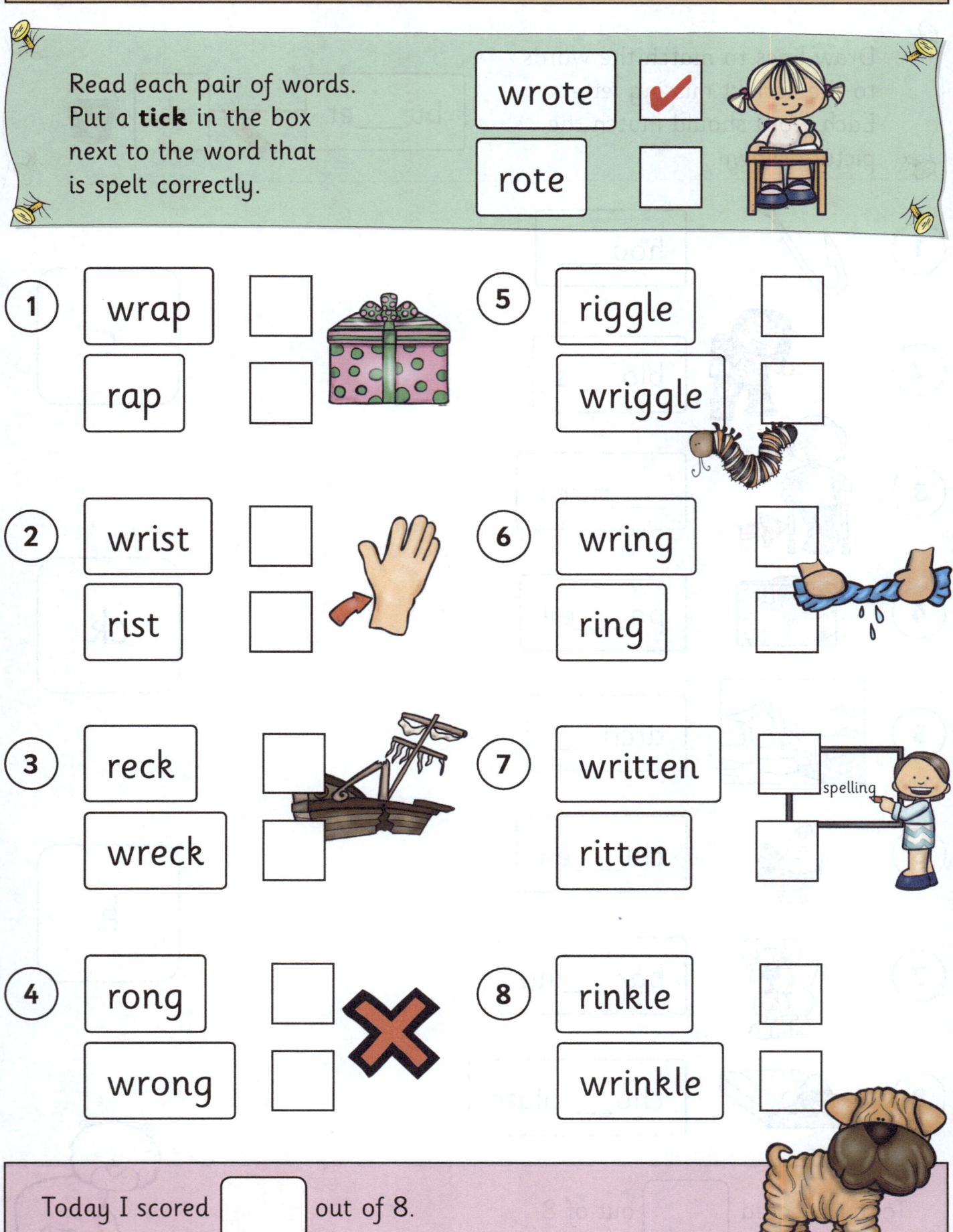

Week 6 — Day 2

Circle '**g**' or '**k**' to complete each word.

__nock   g   (k)

1. __nit   g   k
2. __now   g   k
3. __not   g   k
4. __naw   g   k
5. __nife   g   k
6. __nome   g   k
7. __night   g   k
8. __neepad   g   k

Today I scored [ ] out of 8.

Week 6 — Day 3

Read each sentence. Circle the correct spelling of the word in bold.

What's the story **about** / **abowt**?

1. The wolf had lots of teeth in his **mowth** / **mouth**.

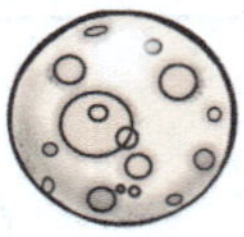

2. He **houled** / **howled** every full moon.

3. The wolf put on a **gown** / **goun**.

4. Red Riding Hood went to the wolf's **house** / **howse**.

5. She was joined by a **couboy** / **cowboy**.

6. The woodcutter was nowhere to be **found** / **fownd**.

Today I scored ☐ out of 6.

Week 6 — Day 4

Fill in the gap with either '**ee**' or '**ea**' to complete each word.

l...ea...n

1) t..........m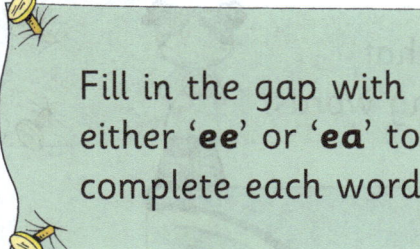

2) g..........se

3) f..........st

4) sh..........p

5) w..........ve

6) ch..........ky

7) fr..........ze

8) scr..........m

9) t..........cup

10) s..........saw

Today I scored ☐ out of 10.

Week 6 — Day 5

Look at the picture below. The sentences describe what is happening. Circle the correct spelling of the missing words.

1. There's a _____ in the sky.   rainboe   rainbow

2. George is picking a _____.   blackberry   blakbery

3. A man is selling _____.   popcorn   poppcorn

4. No one is using the _____.   playgrownd   playground

5. The field is full of _____.   butercups   buttercups

Today I scored ☐ out of 5.

Week 7 — Day 1

Read each sentence. Circle the correct spelling of the missing word.

Lucas could hear the ____ buzzing.   flighs   (flies)

1. The ____ went off.   lite   light

2. It gave Lucas a ____.   friet   fright

3. "It's scary!" he ____.   cried   crighed

4. "Hold my hand ____."   tite   tight

5. "We can give the monster our ____."   frighs   fries

6. "It ____ like some ketchup too."   might   mite

7. It suddenly got ____ again.   briet   bright

8. Lucas let out a ____.   sie   sigh

Today I scored ☐ out of 8.

Week 7 — Day 2

Colour the picture next to the word that is spelt correctly.

1. apple / appal
2. towle / towel
3. tunnal / tunnel
4. animal / animle
5. hospital / hospitel
6. camal / camel

Today I scored ☐ out of 6.

Week 7 — Day 3

Read each sentence, then circle the correct spelling of the word in bold.

We are (going) / goinng to have fun today.

1) We were **playing / playying** at the park.

2) We **kicked / kickked** our football.

3) Suddenly it was **raininng / raining**.

4) The rain was **lashing / lashhing** down.

5) We **startted / started** walking home.

6) The birds were **flyying / flying** to their nests.

7) When we got home we did some **singing / singging**.

8) Mum and Dad **joinned / joined** in.

Today I scored ☐ out of 8.

Week 7 — Day 4

Read each pair of sentences. Tick the sentence where the word in bold is spelt correctly.

✓ The story was full of **peril**.
☐ The story was full of **peral**.

1. ☐ I have a red **pencil**.
   ☐ I have a red **pencel**.

2. ☐ I found a **fossil**.
   ☐ I found a **fossle**.

3. ☐ The wizard is **eval**.
   ☐ The wizard is **evil**.

4. ☐ I have a pet **gerbil**.
   ☐ I have a pet **gerbal**.

5. ☐ I went to **Brazel**.
   ☐ I went to **Brazil**.

6. ☐ I'm a **puple** at school.
   ☐ I'm a **pupil** at school.

7. ☐ Edie used a **stencil**.
   ☐ Edie used a **stencal**.

8. ☐ It rains in **April**.
   ☐ It rains in **Apral**.

9. ☐ I like **lentle** soup.
   ☐ I like **lentil** soup.

10. ☐ I point to my **nostril**.
    ☐ I point to my **nostral**.

Today I scored ☐ out of 10.

Year 2 Spelling — Autumn Term

Week 7 — Day 5

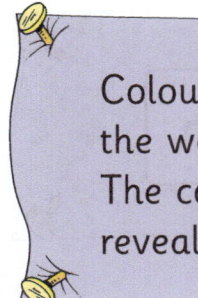

Colour in the squares where the word is spelt correctly. The coloured squares will reveal a hidden letter.

leest	**fear**

leef	dream	teach	leaf	leave	quean
agread	please	speek	teath	streem	creem
nead	cream	agreed	each	team	lieve
eech	leeve	cheet	pleese	teeth	dreem
teem	queen	speak	stream	need	teech

The hidden letter is: ....

Today I scored ☐ out of 15.

Week 8 — Day 1

Read each pair of words. Circle the word that is spelt correctly.

(reach) riech

1. seet | seat

2. feald | field

3. clean | clien

4. pixie | pixea

5. meen | mean

6. squeak | squiek

7. believe | beleave

8. cheaf | chief

Today I scored ☐ out of 8.

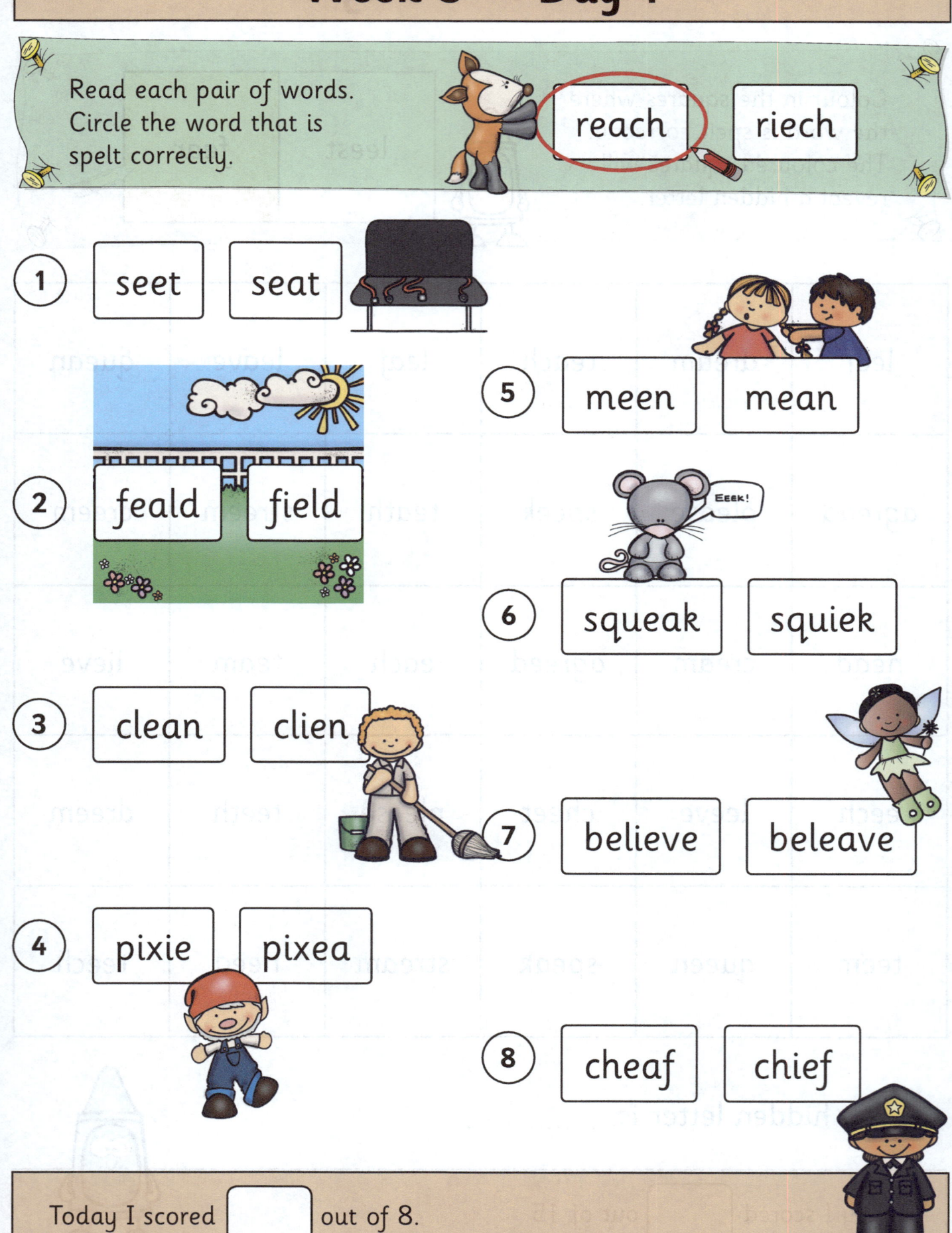

Week 8 — Day 2

Put a ✔ in the box if the word is spelt correctly.
Put a ✘ if it is not spelt correctly.

spie ✘

1. try
2. fri
3. sky
4. fli
5. whigh
6. butterfly
7. reply
8. supplie
9. magnifi
10. multiply

Today I scored ☐ out of 10.

Week 8 — Day 3

Read each sentence. Circle the letters that are missing from the word in bold.

The **Ear___** goes around the Sun.   sh   ch   (th)

1) Rebecca's birthday is on the **four___** of May.   ch   th   sh

2) Kai is trying a new **___ampoo**.   ch   th   sh

3) Danny's body cast a **___adow**.   ch   th   sh

4) Emma is the new **___ampion**.   ch   th   sh

5) Kenji found a **fea___er**.   ch   th   sh

6) Mike is a keen **ar___er**.   ch   th   sh

Today I scored [ ] out of 6.

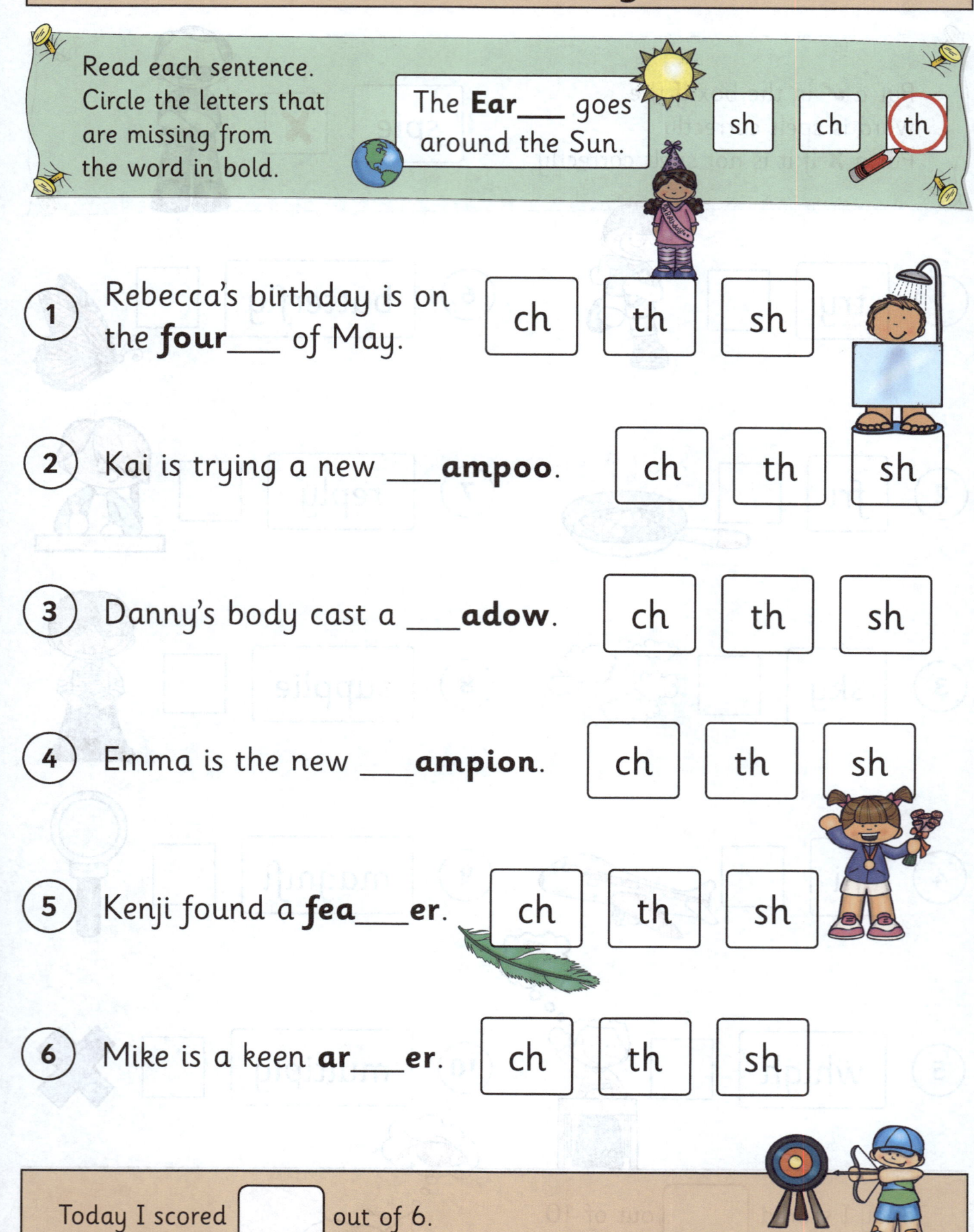

Week 8 — Day 4

Draw lines to match the words to the correct missing letters. Each word should match the picture.

___ake — sn

1. ___owman — sm
2. ___arf — sh
3. ___amp — sc
4. ___oking — sp
5. ___arrow — sw
6. ___ilful — sn
7. ___ield — sl
8. ___ippers — sk

Today I scored ___ out of 8.

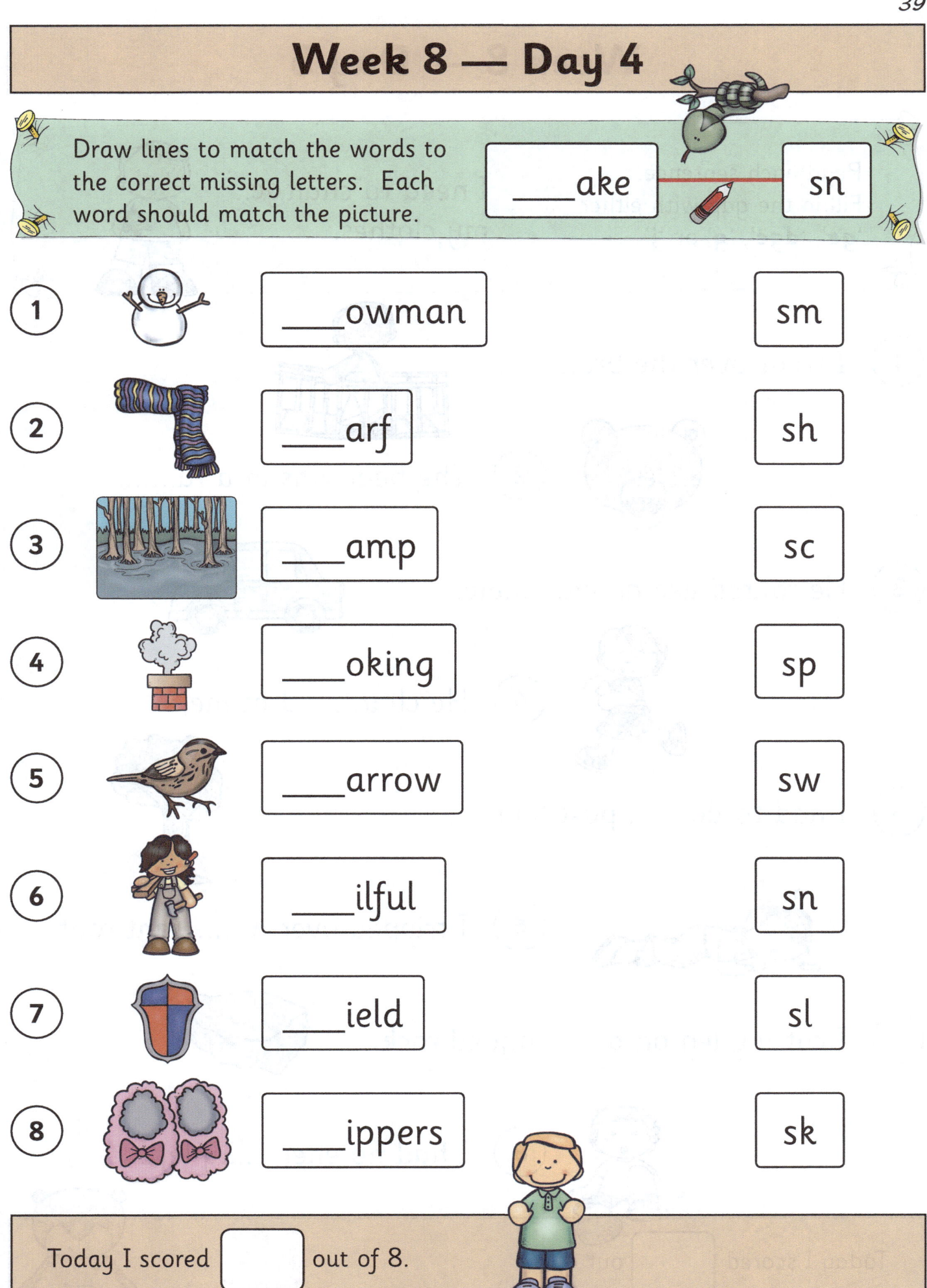

Week 8 — Day 5

Read each sentence. Fill in the gap with either 'ge', 'dge', 'g' or 'j'.

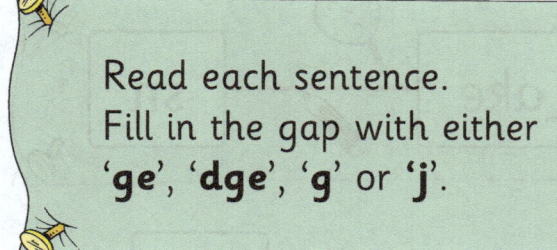

I need to chan.ge.. my clothes.

1) I went over the bri......... .

2) The bear was in a ra......... .

3) He roared like an en.......ine.

4) He char.......d at me.

5) I had to do....... past him.

6) I tripped over a ....iant root.

7) I cut my leg on a ....agged rock.

8) I had no ener.......y left.

Today I scored ☐ out of 8.

Week 9 — Day 1

Draw lines to match the sentences to the correct missing letters.

I have **sp**____ a long time brushing my teeth.

ent

1) I am going to the **dent**____.

unt

2) He will **co**____ my teeth.

est

3) I **alm**____ lost my wobbly tooth.

ast

4) It's a tooth at the **fr**____.

ost

5) I **sugg**____ that it's time to go home.

ont

6) Mum says we will be **go**____ soon.

ist

7) At **le**____ I will get a sticker.

ing

Today I scored ☐ out of 7.

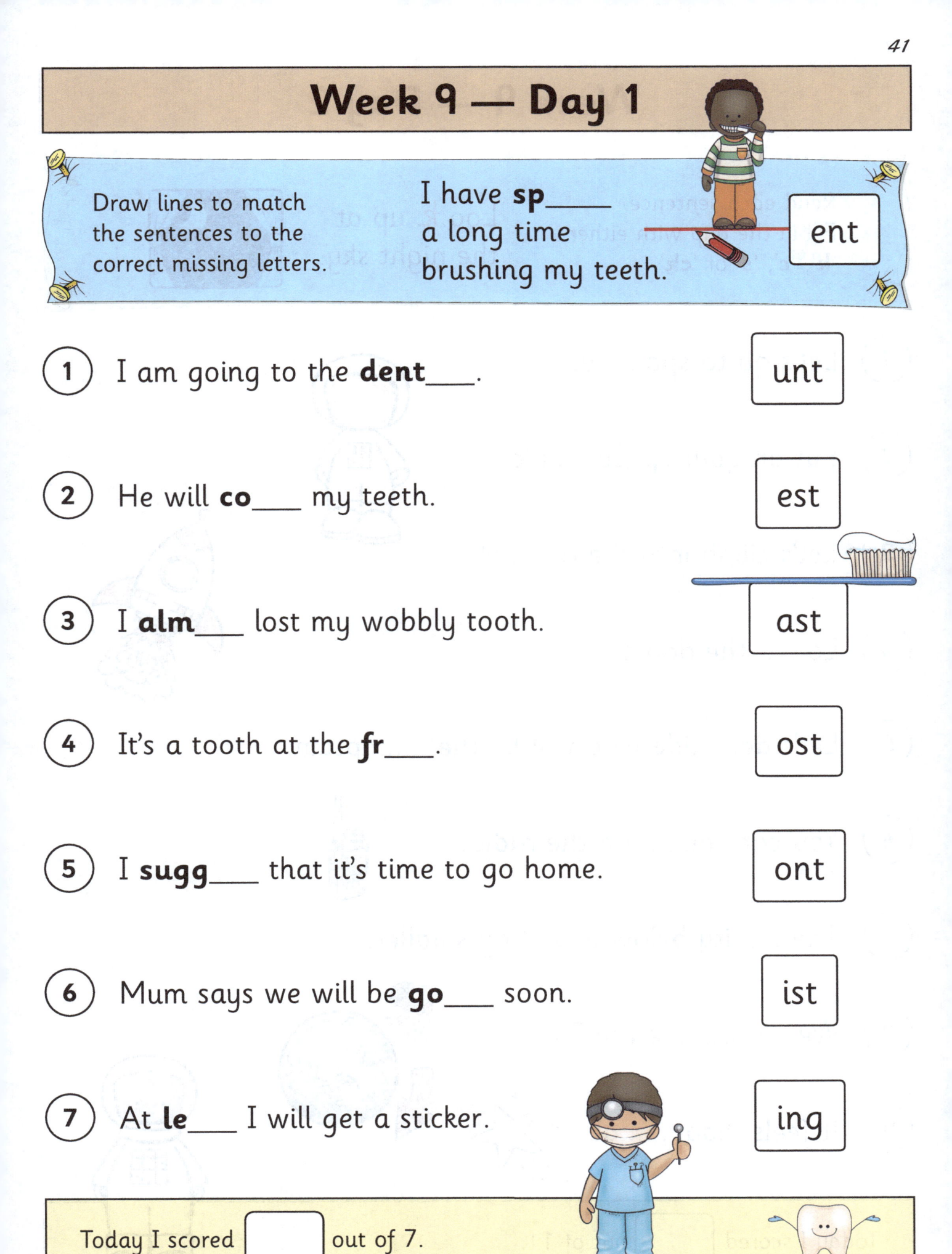

Week 9 — Day 2

Read each sentence.
Fill in the gap with either
'**k**', '**c**', '**s**' or '**ck**'.

Loo.**k**. up at the night sky.

1) Let's go to spa......e.

2) Put on your space......uit.

3) Let's climb into the ro......et.

4) Lo...... the doors.

5) Let's de......ide who will be the ......aptain.

6) You can tal...... on the radio.

7) The ......ity below is getting smaller.

8) We ......ir......le the Earth.

9) It feels magi.......al.

Today I scored [ ] out of 11.

Year 2 Spelling — Autumn Term

Week 9 — Day 3

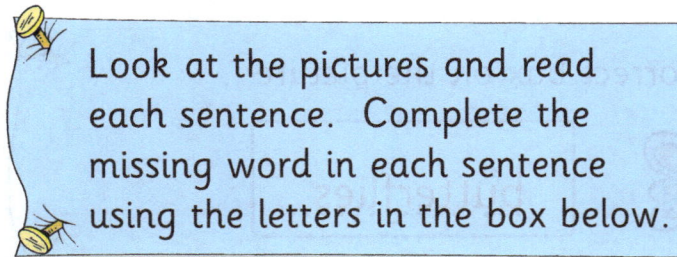

Look at the pictures and read each sentence. Complete the missing word in each sentence using the letters in the box below.

Pirate ships often have **p**.lanks..

~~a n l s k~~

1. Here are some pirate **s**........................

   p i h s

2. The pirates are wearing **h**........................

   s a t

3. They fly **f**........................

   a l s g

4. They use a **c**........................

   s p o m s a

5. Sometimes they wear a **p**........................

   a h c t

6. The boy **w**........................ the deck.

   s e a h s

Today I scored [ ] out of 6.

Week 9 — Day 4

Write the plural of each word in the correct box on the picture.

butterfly   butterflies

1. daddy   3. lady   5. bunny
2. family   4. baby   6. teddy

Today I scored ☐ out of 6.

Week 9 — Day 5

Write the correct spelling of each word in bold to complete the crossword.

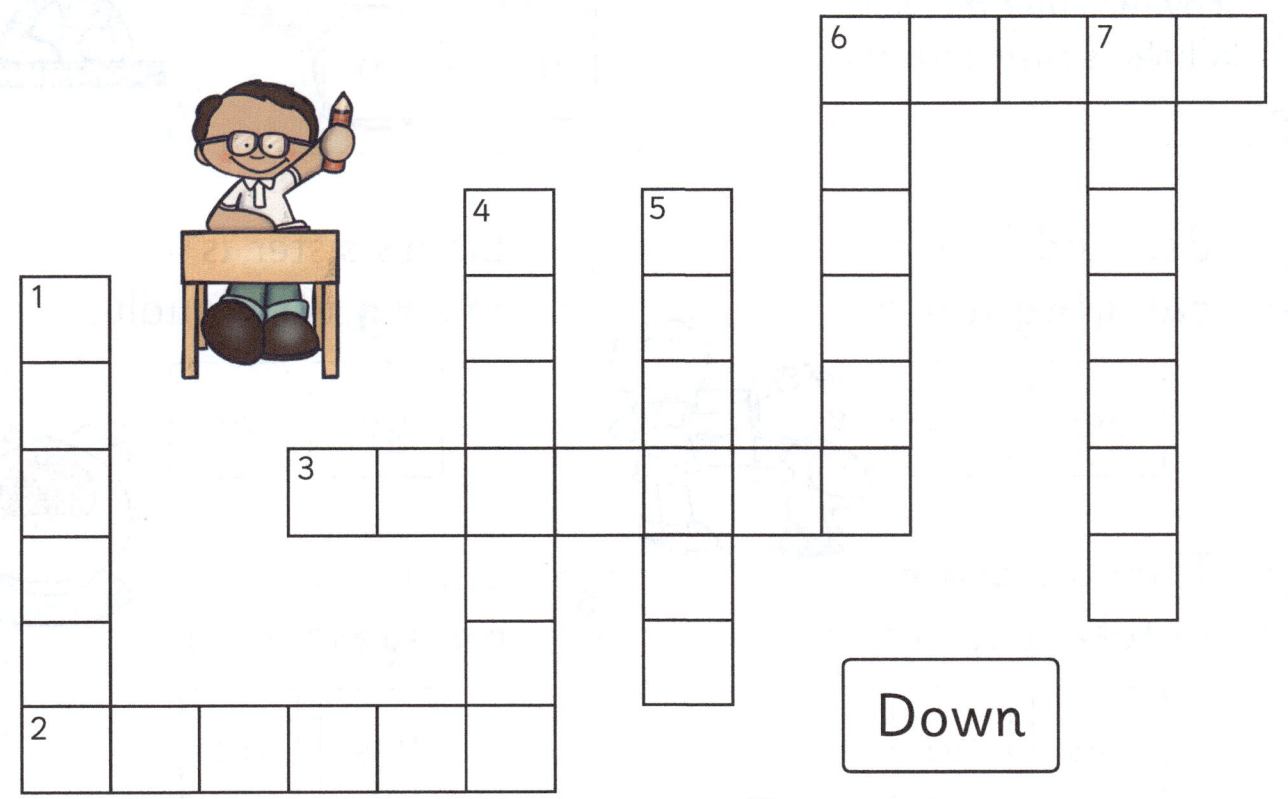

Across

2) Luke **sprayes** water with the toy.

3) Tom **worrys** about the test.

6) Aly **crys** when her mum goes.

Down

1) Mel **enjoyes** reading.

4) Abdul **hurrys** to put on his coat.

5) Joy **tidys** the books.

6) Lisa carefully **copys** her spellings.

7) Abi **emptys** the crayon pot.

Today I scored ☐ out of 8.

Week 10 — Day 1

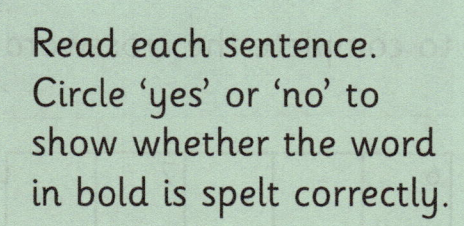

Read each sentence. Circle 'yes' or 'no' to show whether the word in bold is spelt correctly.

I am **replyng** to a letter.

yes | (no)

1. Ben and Jess are **carrying** a box.

   yes | no

2. They are **trying** to take it to school.

   yes | no

3. Francis **hurryed** to clean his room.

   yes | no

4. He is the **tidiest** person I know.

   yes | no

5. Liam's sister is **crying** very loudly.

   yes | no

6. She is the **noisyest** baby.

   yes | no

7. Mya is **worried** that she will miss the bus.

   yes | no

8. She was **playng** with her toys for too long.

   yes | no

Today I scored ☐ out of 8.

Week 10 — Day 2

Read each sentence. Circle the correct spelling of the word in bold.

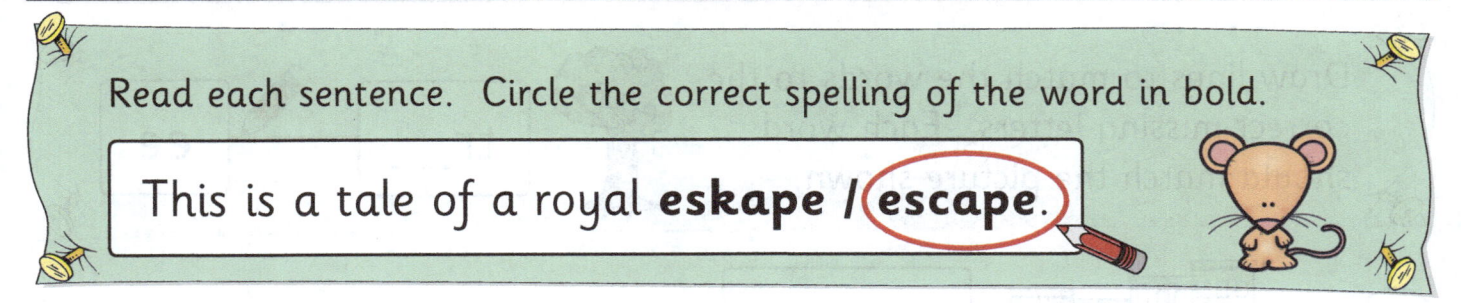

This is a tale of a royal **eskape / escape**.

1) In a faraway land, lived **Prinse / Prince** Paul.

2) He lived in a very large **castle / kastle**.

3) It was a **fancy / fansy** home, but he was lonely.

4) His only friends were some **mise / mice**.

5) They lived in the **cracs / cracks** in the walls.

6) Paul decided to sneak away to the **city / sity**.

7) He left his fine clothes and his **crown / krown** behind.

8) He wore a big **cloack / cloak** and hid in the shadows.

9) He pulled up the hood to hide his **face / fase**.

10) One mouse travelled with him in his **pocket / poket**.

Today I scored ☐ out of 10.

Week 10 — Day 3

Draw lines to match the words to the correct missing letters. Each word should match the picture shown.

tr__ — ee

1. str__t
2. l__t
3. l__f
4. h__t
5. th__f
6. fl__t
7. fr__d
8. sl__p

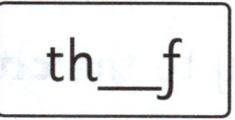

ie
ee
igh
ea

Today I scored ☐ out of 8.

Week 10 — Day 4

Add '**er**' to the words in the boxes to complete the sentences below.

Sam is ......*funnier*...... than Irene. | funny

1) The bee is .... than the snail. | busy

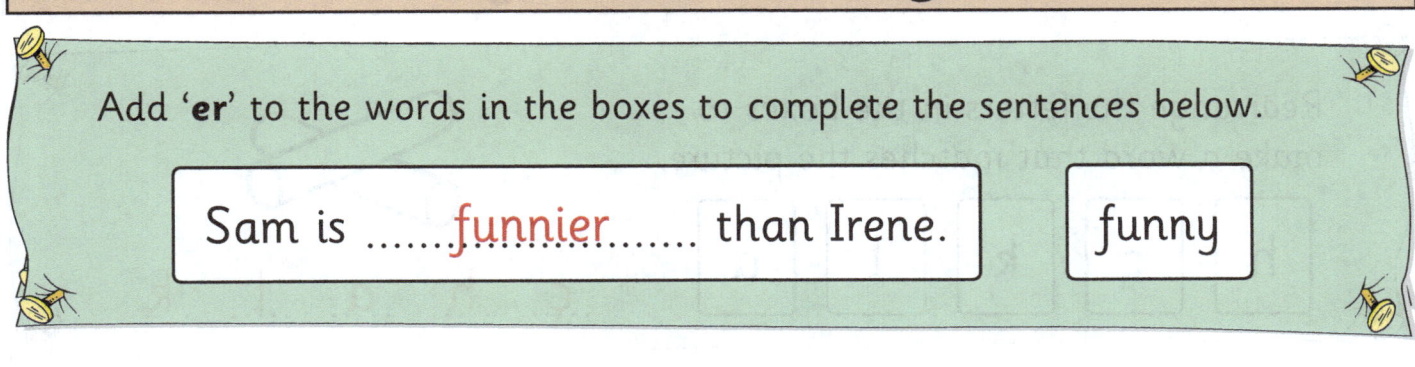

2) Cecil is .... than Rana. | messy

3) Today is .... than yesterday. | sunny

4) A piano is .... than a feather. | heavy

5) Varsha is .... than Ash. | lucky

6) The dog is .... than the rabbit. | noisy

7) My shoes are .... than my slippers. | dirty

8) Destiny is .... than Wayne. | hungry

Today I scored [ ] out of 8.

Week 10 — Day 5

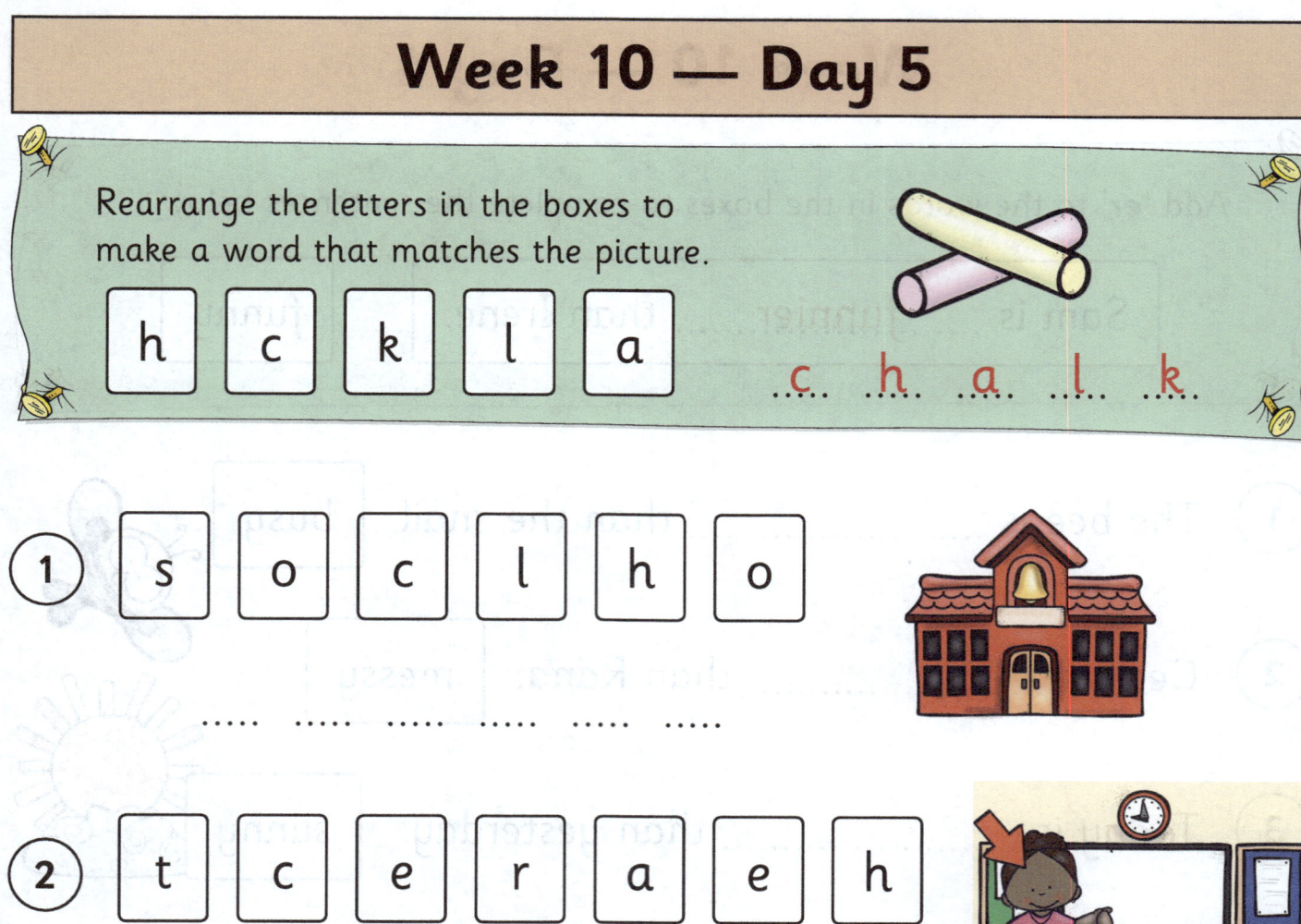

Rearrange the letters in the boxes to make a word that matches the picture.

h c k l a → c h a l k

1) s o c l h o → ....

2) t c e r a e h → ....

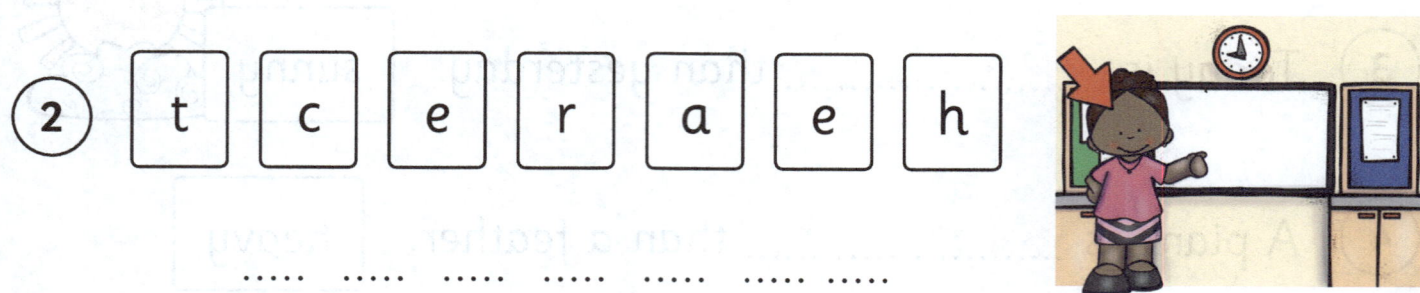

3) n l e i p c → ....

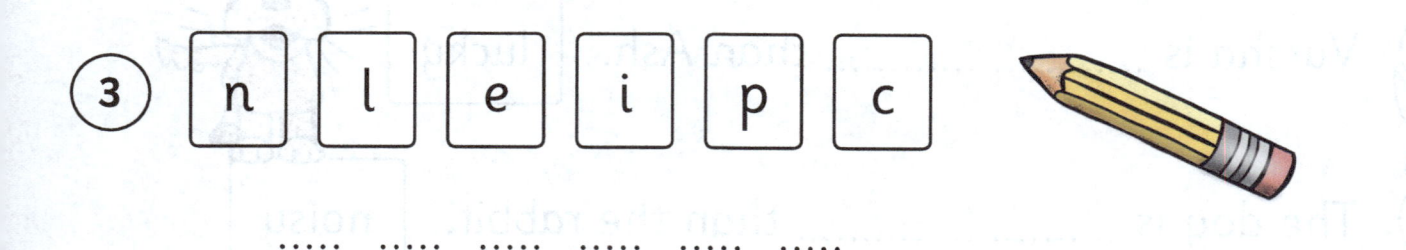

4) i r f e d n s → ....

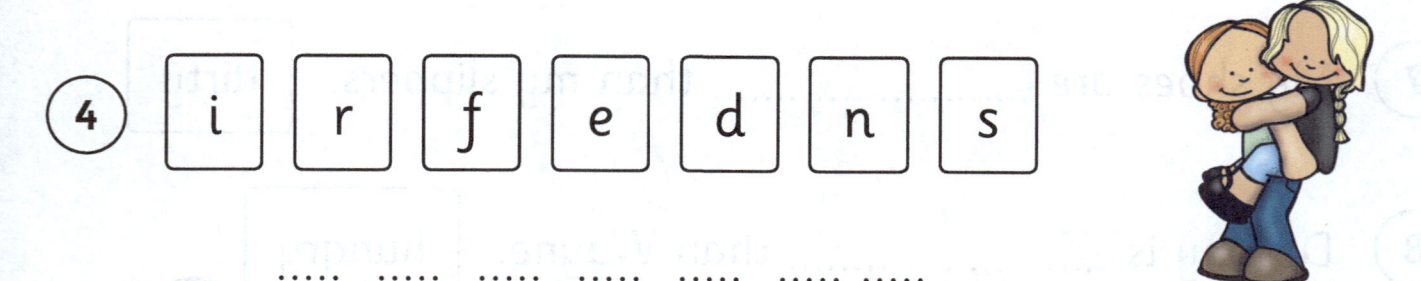

Today I scored ☐ out of 4.

Week 11 — Day 1

Write '**n**', '**gn**' or '**kn**' to complete each word.

.**kn**.itting

1. …..at
2. …..ose
3. …..eck
4. …..uckles
5. …..ame
6. …..ickers
7. …..ee
8. …..aw

Sophie

Today I scored ☐ out of 8.

Week 11 — Day 2

Read each sentence. Add the suffix from the box to the word in bold. Write the new word on the line.

I **wish** I could go to the race. | ed | .wished.

1) They **call** my name. | ed | ....

2) I am feeling **jump**. | y | ....

3) Everyone is **look** at me. | ing | ....

4) I hope I will be the **fast**. | est | ....

5) The starter **shout**, "Get set, go!" | ed | ....

6) I am **think** about the finish. | ing | ....

7) I am feeling **calm** now. | er | ....

8) My dad is the **proud** parent there. | est | ....

Today I scored ☐ out of 8.

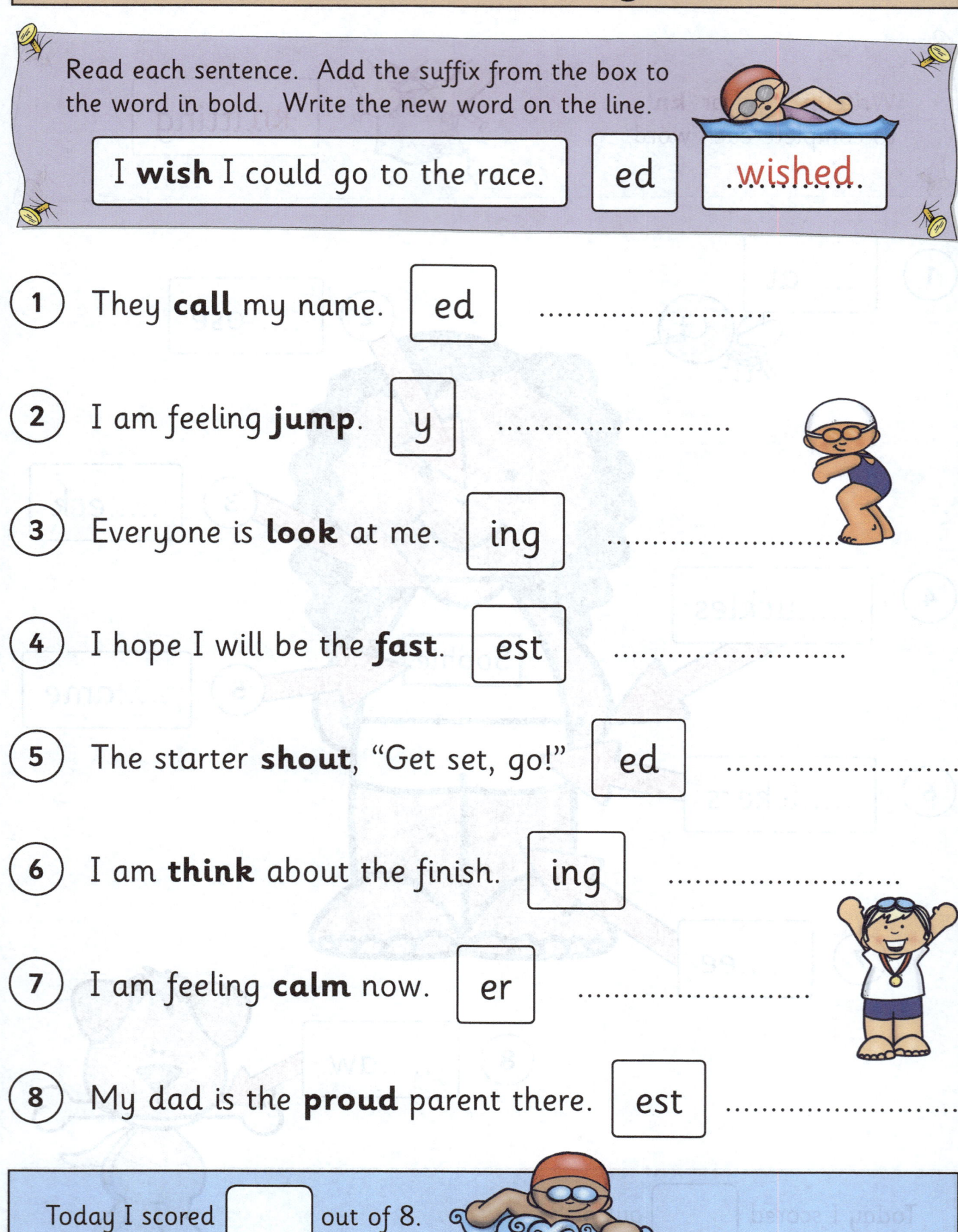

Week 11 — Day 3

Colour in each square where the word is spelt correctly to find the path to the exit.

channel | chanell

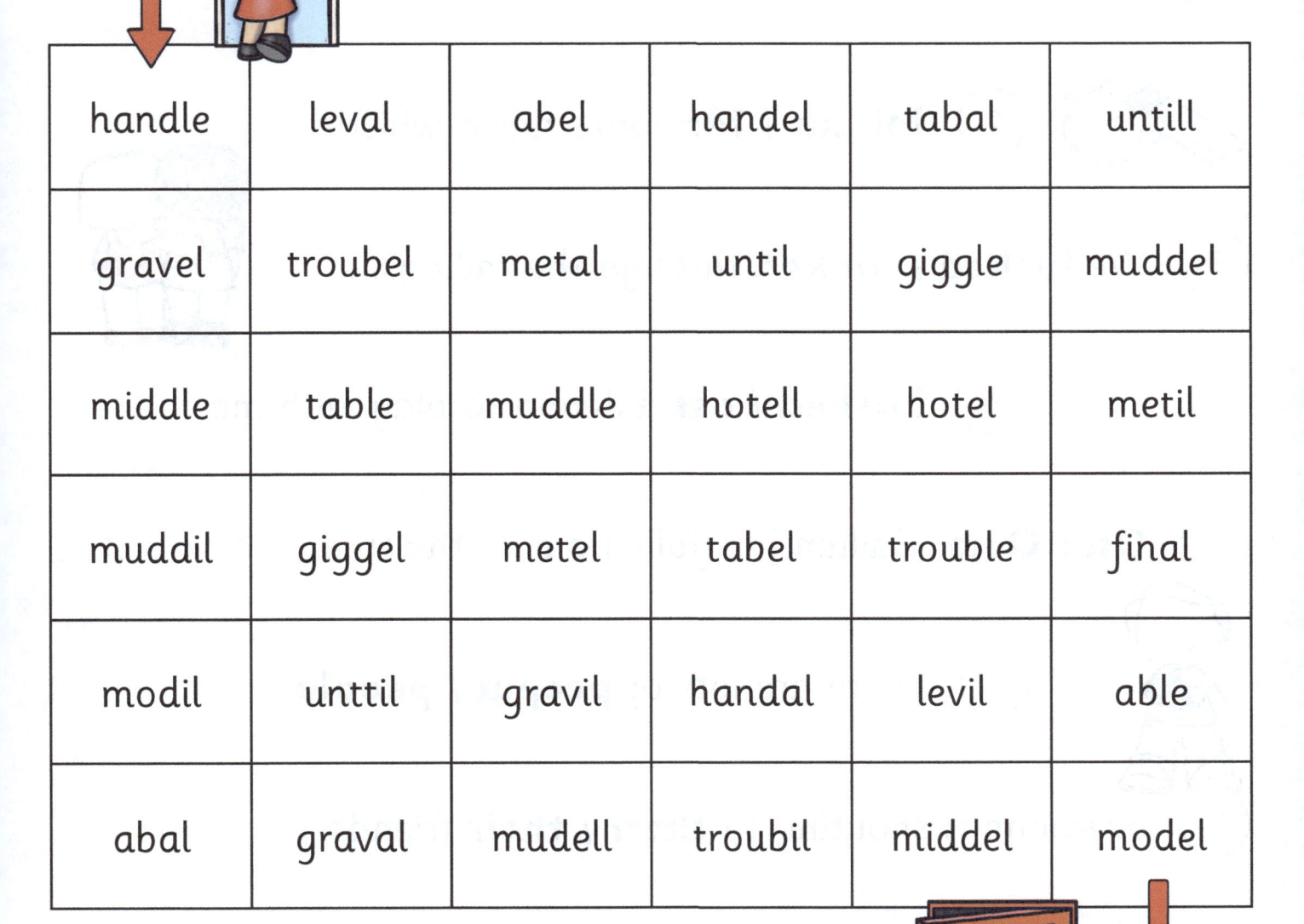

handle	leval	abel	handel	tabal	untill
gravel	troubel	metal	until	giggle	muddel
middle	table	muddle	hotell	hotel	metil
muddil	giggel	metel	tabel	trouble	final
modil	unttil	gravil	handal	levil	able
abal	graval	mudell	troubil	middel	model

Today I scored ☐ out of 13.

Week 11 — Day 4

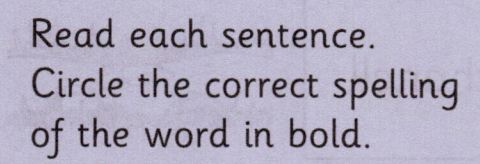

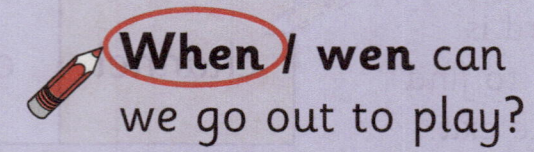

Read each sentence. Circle the correct spelling of the word in bold.

(When) / wen can we go out to play?

1. My teacher is called **Mrs / Misses** Gold.

2. **Mistur / Mr** Jones has a whistle.

3. We **lucked / looked** through the railings.

4. I **asked / askd** Jenna to play with me.

5. **Oh / O** no, Callum has fallen out of the tree.

6. There are lots of **peepul / people**.

7. Everyone is shouting to **therr / their** friends.

8. I think I **could / cud** climb to the top.

Today I scored ☐ out of 8.

Week 11 — Day 5

Look at the word in the first box. Write the correct spelling of the word when the suffix in the second box is added to it.

tame + ed

tamed

1. wide + er

2. hike + ing

3. safe + est

4. smoke + ed

5. shine + y

6. stone + y

7. close + er

8. glide + ing

9. spike + y

10. brave + est

Today I scored ☐ out of 10.

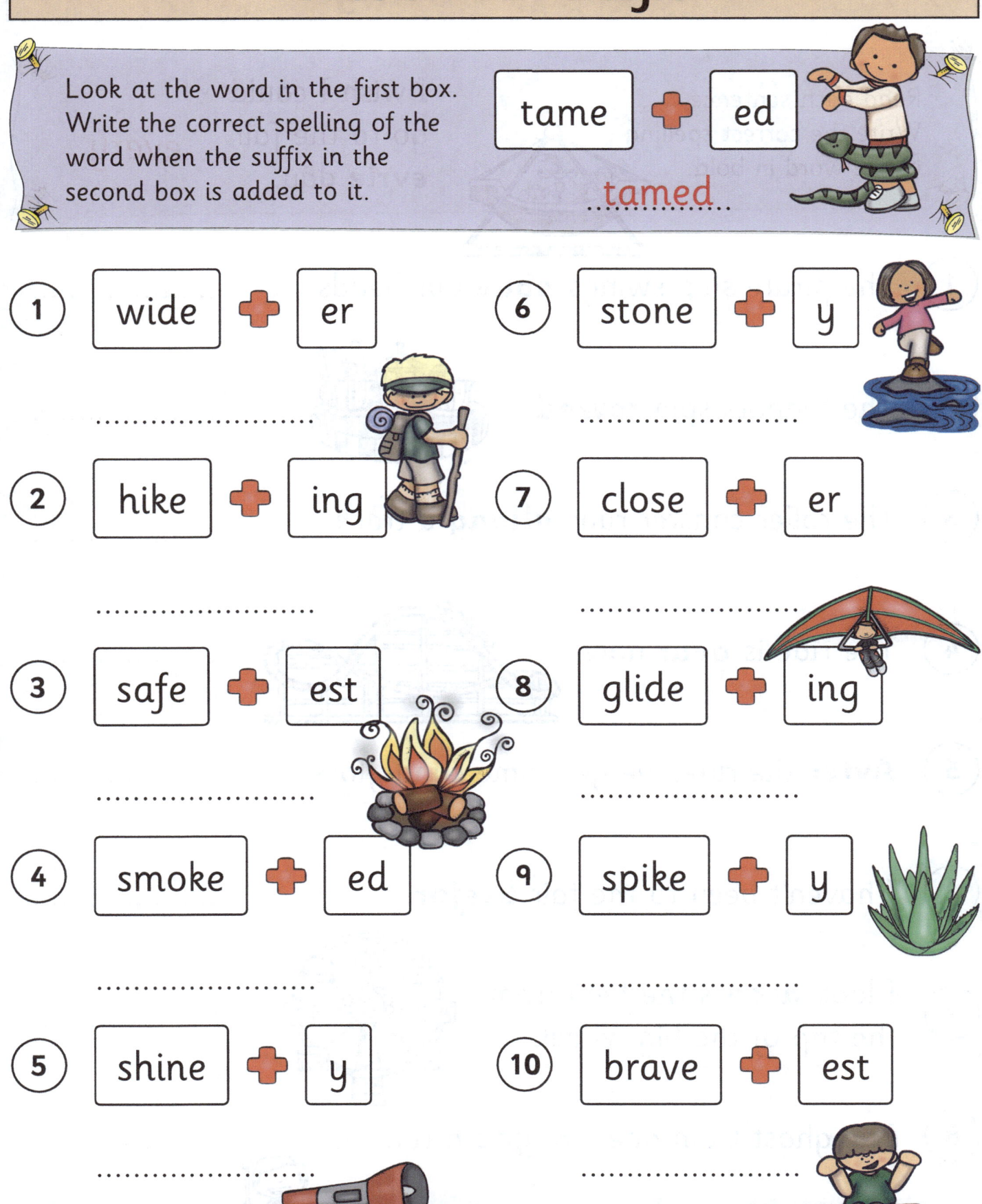

Week 12 — Day 1

Read each sentence. Write the correct spelling of the word in bold.

I wish I could go to the fair **evrie** day. ...every...

1. The pirate ship swings **abuv** our heads. ....

2. The teapots spin **rownd**. ....

3. The roller coaster runs **allong** a track. ....

4. The ride is **ovur** now. ....

5. **Avter** the ride, we get some candyfloss. ....

6. I haven't been to the fair **beefor**. ....

7. I look **accros** the field from the top of the big wheel. ....

8. The ghost train goes **insyde** a tunnel. ....

Today I scored ☐ out of 8.

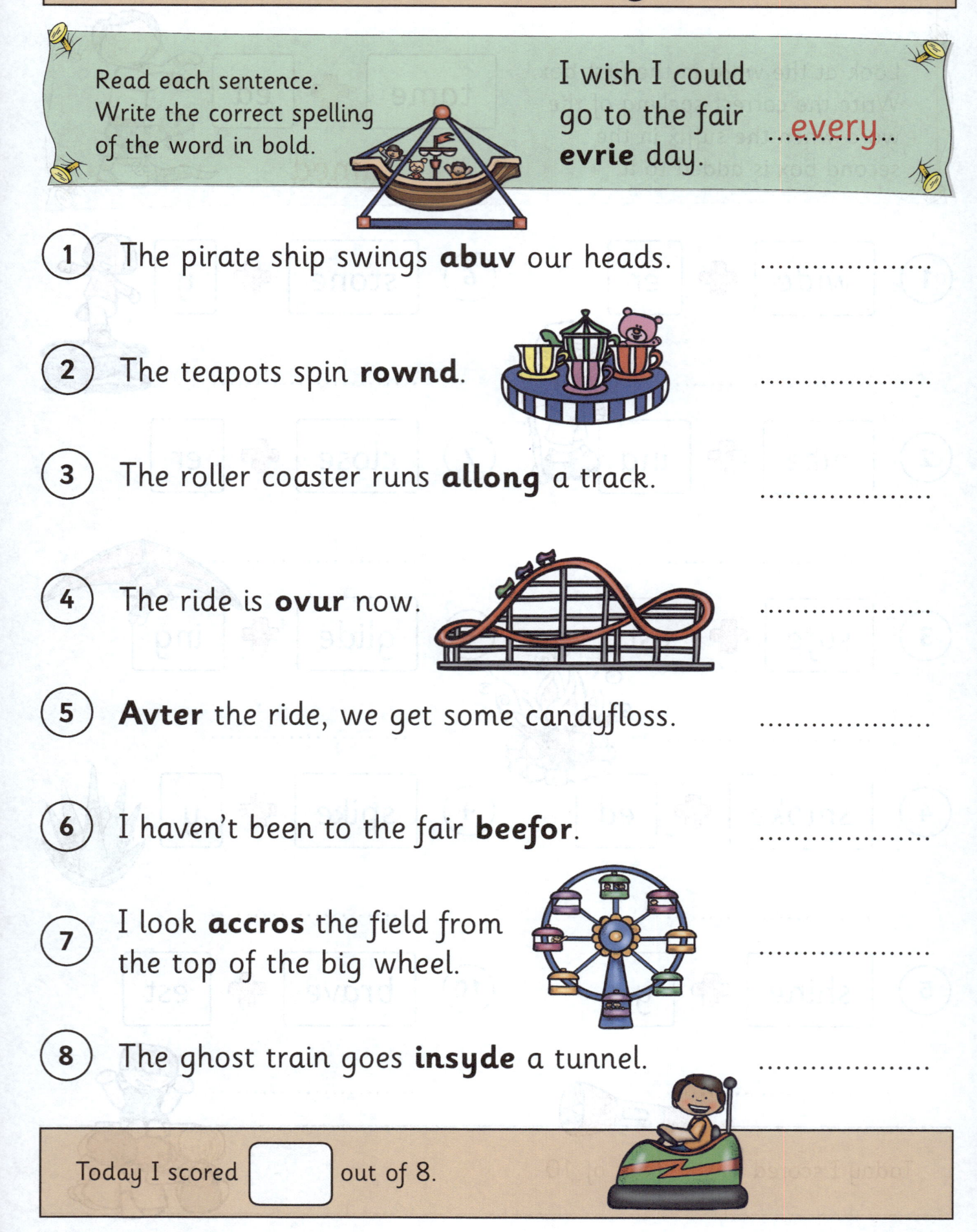

Week 12 — Day 2

Draw lines to match each word with the letter or letters that are missing.

e___e

1. r___t
2. l___s
3. b___e
4. tr___d
5. sp___ing

6. str___pes
7. firef___ter
8. del___t
9. dr___ver
10. n___tmare

y

i

ie

igh

Today I scored [ ] out of 10.

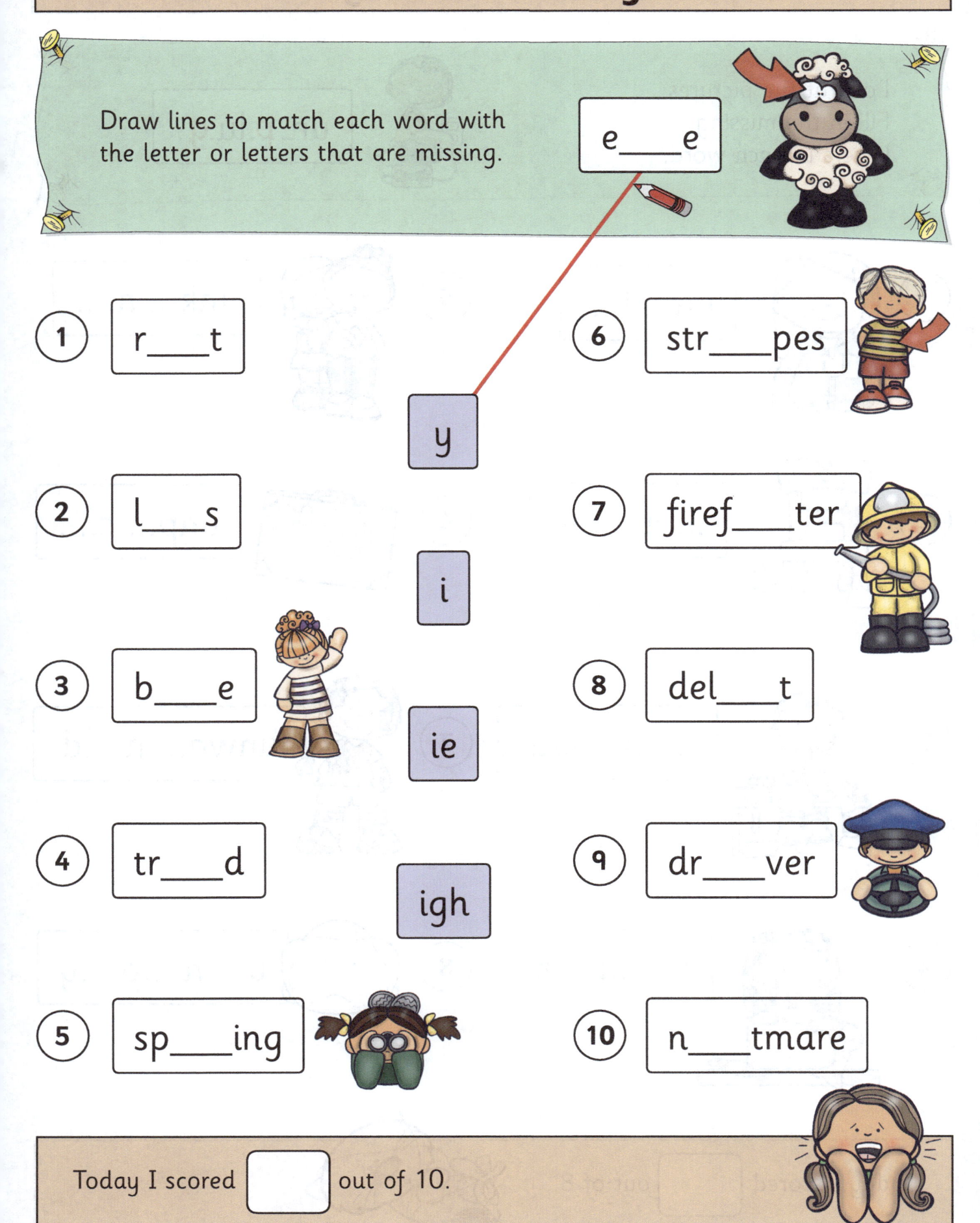

Week 12 — Dav 3

Look at the pictures. Fill in the missing letters in each word.

un.p.lu.g.

1. un....i....

2. ....n....afe

3. ....n....idy

4. un....r....p

5. unk....n....

6. unp....c....

7. unwa....h....d

8. u....h....p....y

Today I scored ☐ out of 8.

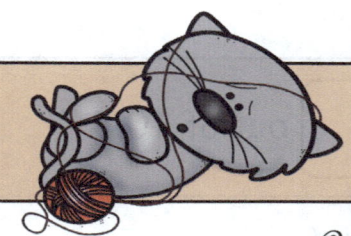

Week 12 — Day 4

Read each sentence. Fill in the gap with either 'wr' or 'r'.

Lucy drops a ...**wr**...**apper**.

1) Casper is ....**iggling**.

2) We are ....**estling**.

3) Tom twists my ....**ist**.

4) Maisy ....**ips** Tom's picture.

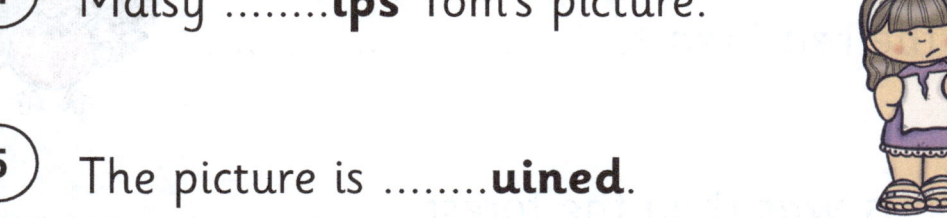

5) The picture is ....**uined**.

6) Mum ....**inkles** her nose because she is cross.

7) "Stop fighting ....**ight** now!" she says.

8) "Sorry, Mum", we ....**eply**.

Today I scored [ ] out of 8.

Week 12 — Day 5

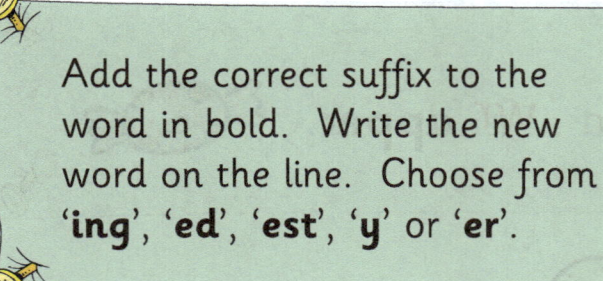

Add the correct suffix to the word in bold. Write the new word on the line. Choose from 'ing', 'ed', 'est', 'y' or 'er'.

Look how high the frog is **hop**! ....hopping....

1. The fox is **sit**. ....

2. The bird **flap**. ....

3. Today it is **sun**. ....

4. The robin has the **red** breast. ....

5. The marsh is **wet** than the forest. ....

6. That is the **fat** cat I've seen! ....

7. Yesterday, the woodpecker **tap** the tree. ....

8. I think it will be even **hot** tomorrow. ....

Today I scored [　] out of 8.

Answers

Week 1 — Day 1
1. I **lo**ve going out.
2. **Give** me my bag.
3. We will be **above** the clouds.
4. It's good to be **active**.
5. We will walk for **twelve** miles.
6. Lots of animals **live** on the mountain.
7. I **forgive** you for splashing me.

Week 1 — Day 2
1. softer
2. sicker
3. calmer
4. sharper
5. wilder
6. stronger
7. darker
8. quicker

Week 1 — Day 3
1. f**oo**d
2. fl**ew**
3. bl**ue**
4. gr**ew**
5. p**oo**l
6. r**oo**t
7. gl**ue**

Week 1 — Day 4
1. Bring some t**oy**s with you.
2. Wh**en** shall we play?
3. Will you pu**sh** me on the swing?
4. He is ca**ll**ed Kamal.
5. He is my fr**ie**nd.
6. Let's have so**me** cake.

Week 1 — Day 5
1. A baby g**ir**l has been born.
2. We are going to ch**ur**ch on Th**ur**sday.
3. It will be my f**ir**st time.
4. Dad washes his sh**ir**t because it is d**ir**ty.
5. I wear my best sk**ir**t and c**ur**l my hair.
6. I do a tw**ir**l.
7. I watch the candle b**ur**n.
8. I'm so happy I could b**ur**st.

Week 2 — Day 1
1. Who will be the fast**est**?
2. The winner is pant**ing**.
3. Milly is the slow**est**.
4. The children are jump**ing**.
5. Theo does the long**est** jump.
6. The children are cheer**ing**.
7. Sports day has end**ed** now.

Week 2 — Day 2
1. It is a sunny day in **June**.
2. The birds are singing a **tune**.
3. It's **time** to go.
4. We go up on the **dune**.
5. We are going to fly my **kite**.
6. It will **rise** up in the air.
7. Then it will **dive** down again.

Week 2 — Day 3
1. The dinos**au**r was hungry.
2. He found some r**aw** meat.
3. His cl**aw**s were sharp.
4. He t**ore** the meat.
5. He cr**aw**led away.
6. Then he y**aw**ned.
7. I heard him sn**ore**.
8. He slept until m**or**ning.

Week 2 — Day 4
1. mummy
2. pretty
3. funny
4. teddy
5. pony
6. happy
7. hurry
8. cosy

Week 2 — Day 5
1. fr**ow**n
2. l**ou**d
3. t**ow**er
4. cr**ou**ch
5. cr**ow**n
6. **ou**tside
7. **ou**ch
8. pr**ou**d

Week 3 — Day 1

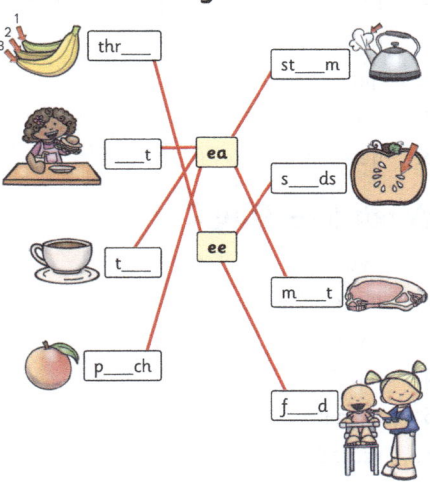

Week 3 — Day 2
1. We are going aw**ay**.
2. We p**ai**d for a ticket.
3. We get on the tr**ai**n.
4. I p**oi**nt out of the window.
5. I can see a b**oy**.
6. He is pl**ay**ing on his bike.
7. M**ay**be one day, I will do tricks like that.
8. I would enj**oy** that very much.

Week 3 — Day 3
1. We went on a (bowt).
2. We could see lots of **fish**.
3. (Thenn) I saw a **shark**.
4. It was (sutch) a **shock**.
5. It **opened** its (mowth).
6. It had (charp) **teeth**.
7. There was a (crashe).
8. I (throo) it one of my **chips**.
9. It **arched** its back and swam off with a (splach).

Week 3 — Day 4
1. **f**rog
2. **wh**ale
3. **z**ebra
4. **g**orilla
5. **d**olphin
6. **h**edgehog
7. **f**lamingo
8. **wh**iskers

Week 3 — Day 5
1. pie
2. hide
3. smile
4. night
5. shine
6. high
7. cried
8. tight

Week 4 — Day 1
1. yes
2. no
3. yes
4. no
5. no
6. yes
7. no
8. yes

Week 4 — Day 2
1. bear
2. glare
3. swear
4. repair
5. unfair
6. scared

Week 4 — Day 3
1. no
2. yes
3. yes
4. no
5. yes
6. no

Week 4 — Day 4
1. r**oa**st
2. g**oes**
3. gr**ow**
4. fl**oa**t
5. tipt**oe**
6. sn**ow**
7. cockr**oa**ch

Week 4 — Day 5
1. sledge
2. bulge
3. dodge
4. ginger
5. change
6. fridge

Week 5 — Day 1
1. ra**ce**
2. noi**se**
3. spi**ce**
4. sli**ce**
5. chan**ce**
6. chee**se**

Week 5 — Day 2
1. yes
2. yes
3. no
4. no
5. yes
6. no

Week 5 — Day 3
1. spa**ce**
2. jui**ce**
3. nur**se**
4. goo**se**
5. voi**ce**
6. cha**se**d
7. choi**ce**

Week 5 — Day 4
1. bl**ue**
2. h**oo**t
3. st**ew**
4. br**ew**
5. pr**oo**f
6. resc**ue**
7. scr**ew**s
8. stat**ue**
9. T**ue**sday
10. ball**oo**n

Week 5 — Day 5
1. hoo**k**
2. blo**ck**s
3. **c**rutch
4. pa**ck**ed
5. arcti**c**
6. chi**ck**en
7. bar**k**ing
8. **ch**ocolate

Week 6 — Day 1
1. **w**rap
2. **w**rist
3. **w**reck
4. **w**rong
5. **w**riggle
6. **w**ring
7. **w**ritten
8. **w**rinkle

Week 6 — Day 2
1. **k**nit
2. **k**now
3. **k**not
4. **g**naw
5. **k**nife
6. **g**nome
7. **k**night
8. **k**neepad

Week 6 — Day 3
1. The wolf had lots of teeth in his **mouth**.
2. He **howled** every full moon.
3. The wolf put on a **gown**.
4. Red Riding Hood went to the wolf's **house**.
5. She was joined by a **cowboy**.
6. The woodcutter was nowhere to be **found**.

Week 6 — Day 4
1. t**ea**m
2. g**ee**se
3. f**ea**st
4. sh**ee**p
5. w**ea**ve
6. ch**ee**ky
7. fr**ee**ze
8. scr**ea**m
9. t**ea**cup
10. s**ee**saw

Week 6 — Day 5
1. rainbow
2. blackberry
3. popcorn
4. playground
5. buttercups

Answers

Week 7 — Day 1
1. light
2. fright
3. cried
4. tight
5. fries
6. might
7. bright
8. sigh

Week 7 — Day 2
1. apple
2. towel
3. tunnel
4. animal
5. hospital
6. camel

Week 7 — Day 3
1. We were **playing** at the park.
2. We **kicked** our football.
3. Suddenly it was **raining**.
4. The rain was **lashing** down.
5. We **started** walking home.
6. The birds were **flying** to their nests.
7. When we got home we did some **singing**.
8. Mum and Dad **joined** in.

Week 7 — Day 4
1. I have a red **pencil**.
2. I found a **fossil**.
3. The wizard is **evil**.
4. I have a pet **gerbil**.
5. I went to **Brazil**.
6. I'm a **pupil** at school.
7. Edie used a **stencil**.
8. It rains in **April**.
9. I like **lentil** soup.
10. I point to my **nostril**.

Week 7 — Day 5

leef	dream	teach	leaf	leave	quean
agread	please	speek	teath	streem	creem
nead	cream	agreed	each	team	lieve
eech	leeve	cheet	pleese	teeth	dreem
teem	queen	speak	stream	need	teech

The hidden letter is: S

Week 8 — Day 1
1. seat
2. field
3. clean
4. pixie
5. mean
6. squeak
7. believe
8. chief

Week 8 — Day 2
1. ✔
2. ✘
3. ✔
4. ✘
5. ✘
6. ✔
7. ✔
8. ✘
9. ✘
10. ✔

Week 8 — Day 3
1. Rebecca's birthday is on the four**th** of May.
2. Kai is trying a new **sh**ampoo.
3. Danny's body cast a **sh**adow.
4. Emma is the new **ch**ampion.
5. Kenji found a fea**th**er.
6. Mike is a keen ar**ch**er.

Week 8 — Day 4
1. **sn**owman
2. **sc**arf
3. **sw**amp
4. **sm**oking
5. **sp**arrow
6. **sk**ilful
7. **sh**ield
8. **sl**ippers

Week 8 — Day 5
1. I went over the bri**dge**.
2. The bear was in a ra**ge**.
3. He roared like an en**g**ine.
4. He char**g**ed at me.
5. I had to do**dge** past him.
6. I tripped over a **g**iant root.
7. I cut my leg on a **j**agged rock.
8. I had no ener**g**y left.

Week 9 — Day 1
1. I am going to the dent**ist**.
2. He will co**unt** my teeth.
3. I alm**ost** lost my wobbly tooth.
4. It's a tooth at the fr**ont**.
5. I sugg**est** that it's time to go home.
6. Mum says we will be go**ing** soon.
7. At le**ast** I will get a sticker.

Week 9 — Day 2
1. Let's go to spa**ce**.
2. Put on your space**s**uit.
3. Let's climb into the ro**ck**et.
4. Lo**ck** the doors.
5. Let's de**c**ide who will be the **c**aptain.
6. You can tal**k** on the radio.
7. The **c**ity below is getting smaller.
8. We **c**ircle the Earth.
9. It feels magi**c**al.

Week 9 — Day 3
1. Here are some pirate **ships**.
2. The pirates are wearing **hats**.
3. They fly **flags**.
4. They use a **compass**.
5. Sometimes they wear a **patch**.
6. The boy **washes** the deck.

Week 9 — Day 4
1. daddies
2. families
3. ladies
4. babies
5. bunnies
6. teddies

Week 9 — Day 5

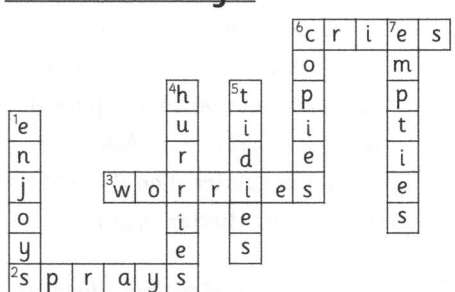

						⁶c	r	i	⁷e	s
						o			m	
			⁴h		⁵t	p			p	
¹e			u		i	d			t	
n			r		d	e			i	
j		³w	o	r	r	i	e	s	e	
o			i		e				s	
y			e		s					
²s	p	r	a	y	s					

Week 10 — Day 1
1. yes
2. yes
3. no
4. yes
5. yes
6. no
7. yes
8. no

Week 10 — Day 2
1. In a faraway land, lived **Prince** Paul.
2. He lived in a very large **castle**.
3. It was a **fancy** home, but he was lonely.
4. His only friends were some **mice**.
5. They lived in the **cracks** in the walls.
6. Paul decided to sneak away to the **city**.
7. He left his fine clothes and his **crown** behind.
8. He wore a big **cloak** and hid in the shadows.
9. He pulled up the hood to hide his **face**.
10. One mouse travelled with him in his **pocket**.

Week 10 — Day 3
1. str**ee**t
2. l**igh**t
3. l**ea**f
4. h**ea**t
5. th**ie**f
6. fl**igh**t
7. fr**ie**d
8. sl**ee**p

Week 10 — Day 4
1. The bee is **busier** than the snail.
2. Cecil is **messier** than Rana.
3. Today is **sunnier** than yesterday.
4. A piano is **heavier** than a feather.
5. Varsha is **luckier** than Ash.
6. The dog is **noisier** than the rabbit.
7. My shoes are **dirtier** than my slippers.
8. Destiny is **hungrier** than Wayne.

Week 10 — Day 5
1. school
2. teacher
3. pencil
4. friends

Week 11 — Day 1
1. **gn**at
2. **n**ose
3. **n**eck
4. **kn**uckles
5. **n**ame
6. **kn**ickers
7. **kn**ee
8. **gn**aw

Week 11 — Day 2
1. called
2. jumpy
3. looking
4. fastest
5. shouted
6. thinking
7. calmer
8. proudest

Week 11 — Day 3

handle	leval	abel	handel	tabal	untill
gravel	troubel	metal	until	giggle	muddel
middle	table	muddle	hotell	hotel	metil
muddil	giggel	metel	tabel	trouble	final
modil	unttil	gravil	handal	levil	able
abal	graval	mudell	troubil	middel	model

(Correct spellings shaded: handle, gravel, metal, until, giggle, middle, table, muddle, hotel, trouble, final, level, able, model)

Week 11 — Day 4
1. My teacher is called **Mrs** Gold.
2. **Mr** Jones has a whistle.
3. We **looked** through the railings.
4. I **asked** Jenna to play with me.
5. **Oh** no, Callum has fallen out of the tree.
6. There are lots of **people**.
7. Everyone is shouting to **their** friends.
8. I think I **could** climb to the top.

Week 11 — Day 5
1. wider
2. hiking
3. safest
4. smoked
5. shiny
6. stony
7. closer
8. gliding
9. spiky
10. bravest

Week 12 — Day 1
1. above
2. round
3. along
4. over
5. After
6. before
7. across
8. inside

Week 12 — Day 2
1. r**igh**t
2. l**ie**s
3. b**ye**
4. tr**ie**d
5. sp**y**ing
6. str**ipe**s
7. firef**igh**ter
8. del**igh**t
9. dr**i**ver
10. n**igh**tmare

Week 12 — Day 3
1. **un**zip
2. **un**safe
3. **un**tidy
4. **un**wrap
5. **un**kind
6. **un**pack
7. **un**washed
8. **un**happy

Week 12 — Day 4
1. Casper is **wr**iggling.
2. We are **wr**estling.
3. Tom twists my **wr**ist.
4. Maisy rips Tom's picture.
5. The picture is ruined.
6. Mum **wr**inkles her nose because she is cross.
7. "Stop fighting right now!" she says.
8. "Sorry, Mum", we reply.

Week 12 — Day 5
1. sitting
2. flapped
3. sunny
4. reddest
5. wetter
6. fattest
7. tapped
8. hotter